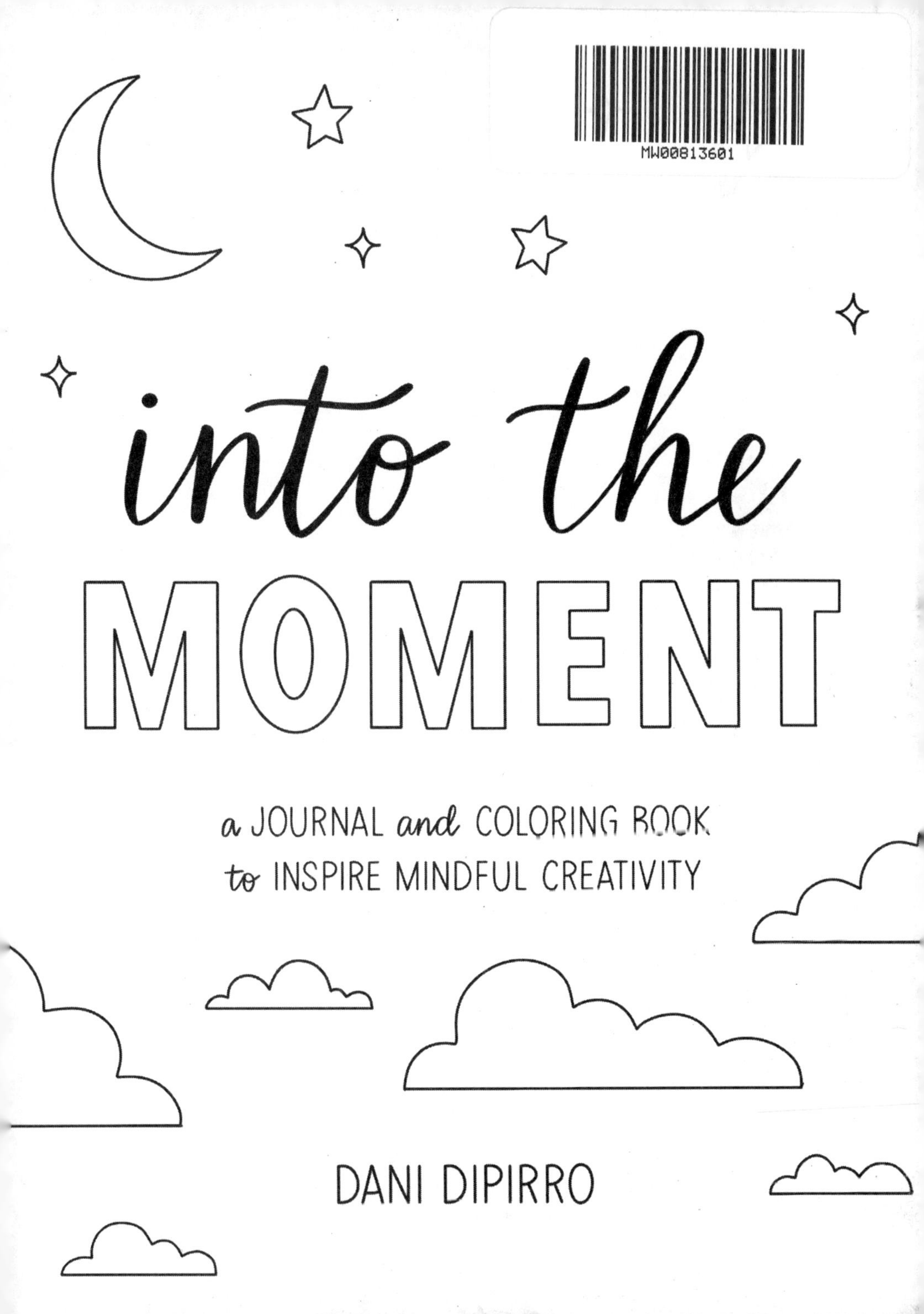
MW00813601
into the
MOMENT
a JOURNAL and COLORING BOOK
to INSPIRE MINDFUL CREATIVITY
DANI DIPIRRO

AN IMPRINT OF PENGUIN RANDOM HOUSE LLC
PENGUINRANDOMHOUSE.COM

TRADE PAPERBACK ISBN: 9780593715338

PRINTED IN CANADA
10 9 8 7 6 5 4 3 2 1

BOOK DESIGN BY DANI DIPIRRO

INTRODUCTION

WELCOME TO INTO THE MOMENT! I'M DANI, AND I DESIGNED THIS BOOK WITH ENGAGING AND INSPIRING ACTIVITIES TO OFFER POSITIVE AND CREATIVE GUIDANCE FOR STAYING PRESENT. AS THE FOUNDER OF POSITIVELY PRESENT, A SPACE DEDICATED TO HELPING OTHERS STAY OPTIMISTIC AND MINDFUL, I'VE SPENT YEARS EXPLORING WAYS TO FACE LIFE'S HIGHS AND LOWS WITH A POSITIVE AND PRESENT ATTITUDE, AND I'VE FOUND THAT ONE OF THE BEST WAYS TO CONNECT WITH THE MOMENT IS THROUGH CREATIVE ACTIVITIES.

TO HELP YOU STAY IN THE MOMENT, I'VE FILLED THIS BOOK WITH WRITING PROMPTS, DRAWING EXERCISES, AND COLORING PAGES CAREFULLY DESIGNED TO AID IN THE DISRUPTION OF RUMINATION, INSPIRE YOU TO PRESS PAUSE ON OVERTHINKING, AND GUIDE YOU BACK TO THE PRESENT. ALL OF THESE HAVE BEEN TESTED BY ME, A NOTORIOUSLY ANXIOUS OVERTHINKER, AND THEY REALLY DO HELP GET ME OUT OF MY HEAD AND INTO THE MOMENT.

YOU CAN USE THIS BOOK WHEN YOU'RE FEELING OVERWHELMED, ANXIOUS, OR STRESSED TO BRING YOU BACK TO THE PRESENT. YOU CAN USE THIS BOOK WHEN YOU'RE HAVING A GREAT DAY AND WANT TO REALLY CONNECT WITH THOSE POSITIVE FEELINGS. WHENEVER YOU CHOOSE TO USE THIS BOOK, IT WILL HELP YOU TO RECONNECT WITH THE NOW THROUGH CREATIVITY AND INSPIRATION. THE ACTIVITIES WILL GUIDE YOU, AND THE QUOTES WILL UPLIFT YOU.

EVERY TIME YOU OPEN THIS BOOK, YOU'RE OFFERING YOUR MIND A CREATIVE OUTLET FOR MEANINGFUL CONNECTION – BOTH WITH THE MOMENT AND WITH YOURSELF. THE PROMPTS AND EXERCISES WILL GUIDE YOUR MIND, AND THE COLORING PAGES WILL INSPIRE SIMPLE BUT EFFECTIVE CREATIVE ACTION. BECAUSE COLORING IS ONE OF THE BEST WAYS TO CREATIVELY CONNECT WITH THE PRESENT, MOST OF THE PAGES (EVEN THOSE NOT INTENDED FOR COLORING) HAVE ELEMENTS THAT CAN BE COLORED IN, GIVING YOU MORE OPPORTUNITIES FOR MINDFUL MOMENTS.

THERE'S NO "RIGHT" WAY TO COMPLETE THE PAGES IN THIS BOOK. ITS PURPOSE IS ONLY TO GUIDE YOUR MIND BACK TO THE MOMENT, INSPIRING YOU A BIT ALONG THE WAY. AS LONG AS YOU'RE CONNECTING YOUR PENCIL (OR PEN OR MARKER, ETC.) TO THE PAGE, YOU'RE DOING IT RIGHT.

YOU'LL FIND THAT CERTAIN COLORING PAGES, QUOTES, AND ACTIVITIES SPEAK TO YOU MORE ON SOME DAYS THAN ON OTHERS. SELECT THE PAGES THAT RESONATE WITH YOU, AND IF YOU STUMBLE UPON SOMETHING THAT FEELS OVERWHELMING, TURN TO ANOTHER PAGE THAT'S MORE ALIGNED WITH YOUR CURRENT STATE OF MIND.

AS YOU ALLOW THESE PAGES TO BRING YOU BACK INTO THE MOMENT, YOU'LL SEE THAT THEY CAN ALSO HELP REDUCE RUMINATION, PROMOTE SELF-AWARENESS, INSPIRE YOUR CREATIVITY, ASSIST YOU IN AVOIDING OVERSTIMULATION, INSTILL A SENSE OF CALM, AND SO MUCH MORE.

ARE YOU READY? LET'S GET INTO THE MOMENT!

LEAVE YOUR WORRIES

AS YOU COLOR IN THIS PAGE, IMAGINE YOURSELF RELEASING YOUR WORRIES THE WAY TREES RELEASE LEAVES. WITH EACH LEAF, VISUALIZE A SPECIFIC WORRY FLOATING AWAY FROM YOU.

WE'RE ALL JUST
FIGURING IT OUT AS
WE GO. YOU DON'T
HAVE TO HAVE ALL
OF THE ANSWERS
RIGHT NOW.

WHAT YOU LOVE

IN THE ROOMS BELOW, WRITE ABOUT (OR DRAW!) SOME ITEMS, PEOPLE, OR IDEAS THAT YOU LOVE. RETURN TO THIS PAGE WHEN YOU NEED A REMINDER OF THE GOOD IN THE WORLD.

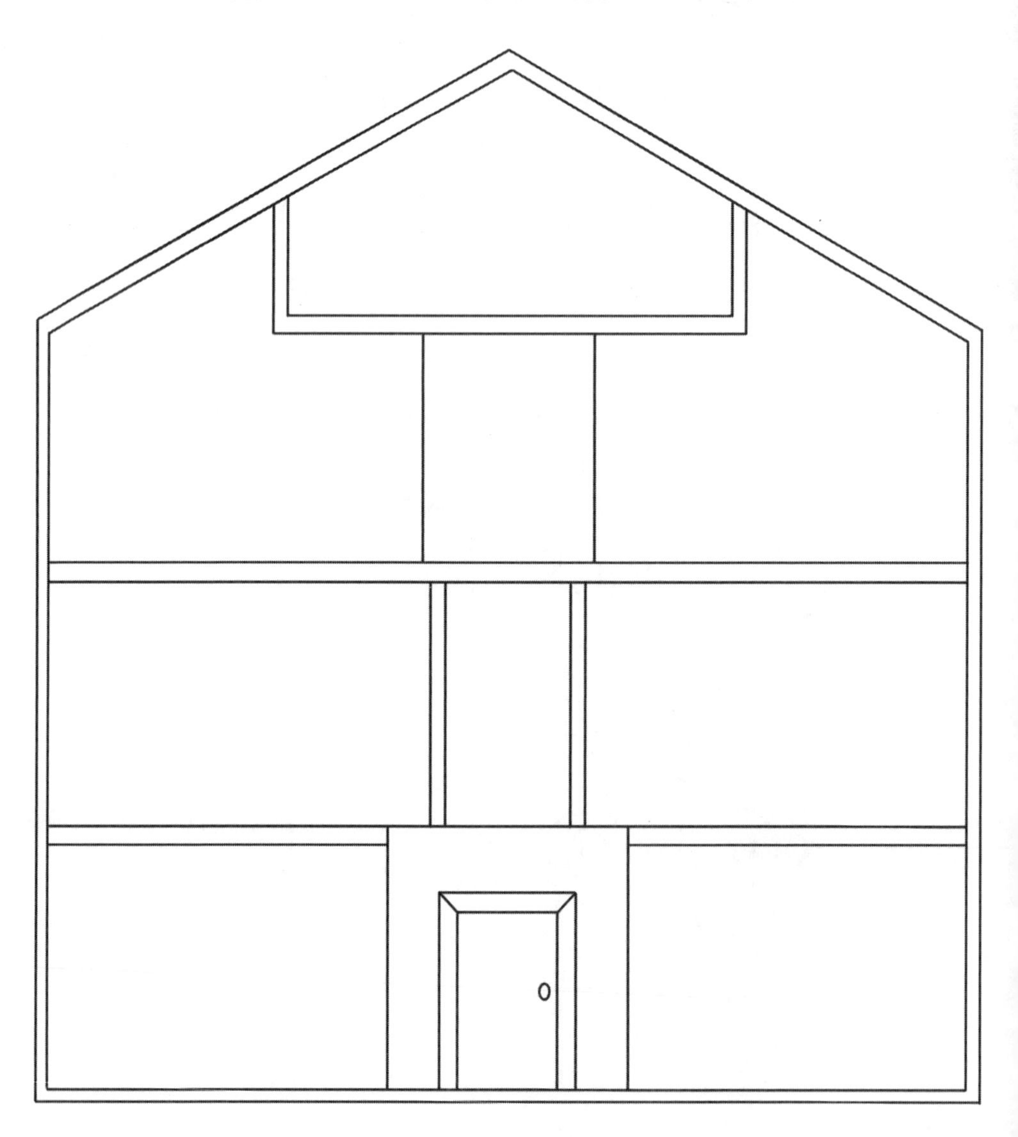

ALLOW
YOURSELF
TO FEEL
HAPPY
WHEN
GOOD
THINGS
HAPPEN.

WHO YOU ARE

WE ALL FEEL DISCONNECTED FROM OURSELVES SOMETIMES. IF YOU'RE FEELING THIS WAY, GET IN TOUCH WITH WHO YOU ARE BY FINISHING THE STATEMENTS BELOW.

I AM A PERSON WHO BELIEVES IN ____________________.

I AM A PERSON WHO WANTS ____________________.

I AM A PERSON WHO ENJOYS ____________________.

I AM A PERSON WHO IS GRATEFUL FOR ____________________.

I AM A PERSON WHO LOVES ____________________.

I AM A PERSON WHO DISLIKES ____________________.

I AM A PERSON WHO CAN ____________________.

I AM A PERSON WHO HASN'T YET ____________________.

I AM A PERSON WHO ALWAYS ____________________.

I AM A PERSON WHO HAS NEVER ____________________.

I AM A PERSON WHO TRIES TO ____________________.

I AM A PERSON WHO WONDERS ABOUT ____________________.

I AM A PERSON WHO IS WAITING FOR ____________________.

LET YOUR FEELINGS
COME AND GO
LIKE CLOUDS
IN THE SKY.

PATTERN PRESENCE

COLOR IN EACH AREA OF THE SHAPE WITH A DIFFERENT PATTERN (STRIPES, PLAID, DOTS, ETC.). FOCUSING ON THE DESIGN WILL BRING YOU BACK TO THE PRESENT MOMENT.

LESS
CRITICIZING,
MORE
CELEBRATING.

FORGET THE TIME

ON THE CLOCKS, WRITE PEOPLE OR ACTIVITIES THAT MAKE YOU FORGET TO CHECK THE TIME. TRY TO ADD MORE OF THESE MINDFUL MOMENTS INTO YOUR DAYS.

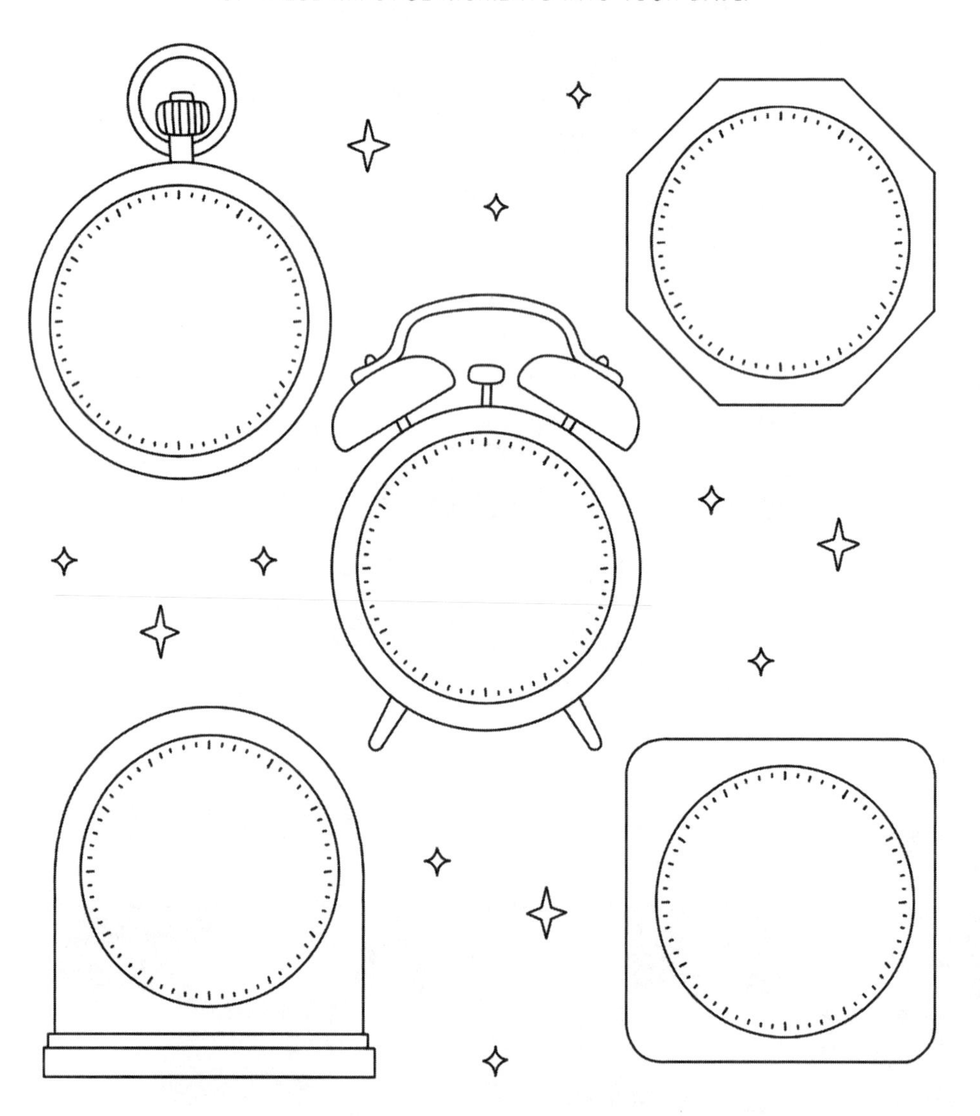

BE ON YOUR
OWN TEAM.
ROOT FOR
YOURSELF.

VERY GOOD ADVICE

WHAT'S SOME OF THE BEST ADVICE YOU'VE EVER RECEIVED (OR GIVEN)? WRITE IT DOWN ON THE NOTES, AND COME BACK TO THIS PAGE WHEN YOU NEED TO BE UPLIFTED OR INSPIRED.

ALL YOU
HAVE TO DO
RIGHT NOW IS
STAY IN THIS
MOMENT.

LUCKY CHARMS

NEXT TO THE LINKS, DRAW SYMBOLS THAT ARE MEANINGFUL TO YOU (OR JUST THINGS YOU LOVE!). THEN KEEP AN EYE OUT FOR THEM IN REAL LIFE. SOME EXAMPLES TO GET YOU STARTED: HEART, CLOVER, STAR, RAINBOW, SUN, FLOWER, ETC.

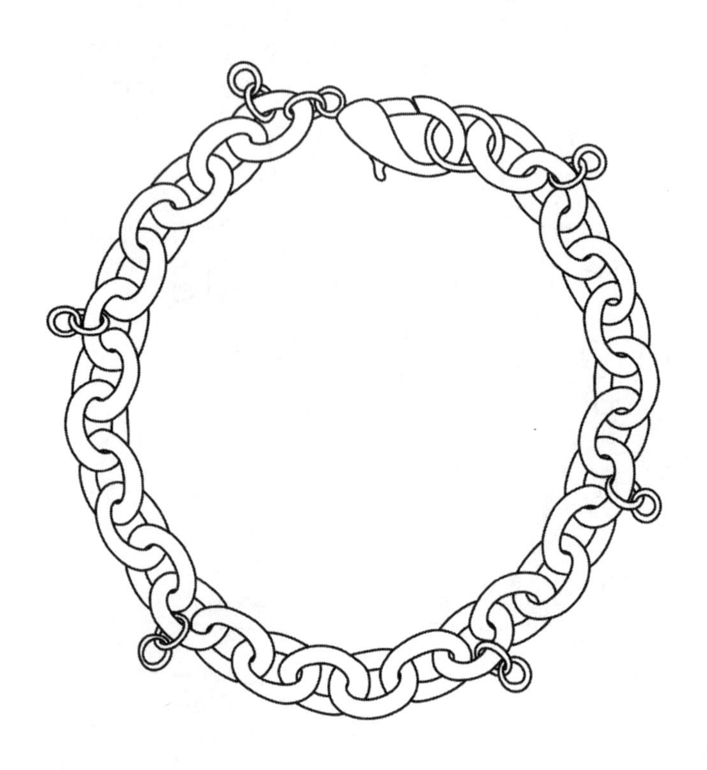

SOME CHAPTERS DON'T NEED TO BE REREAD. IT'S OKAY TO TURN THE PAGE.

ALBUMS ON REPEAT

IN THE SQUARES, DRAW THE COVERS (OR WRITE THE NAMES) OF ALBUMS YOU LOVE. OR DRAW IMAGINARY COVERS FOR ALBUMS YOU'D LIKE TO HEAR. (BONUS: TURN ON YOUR FAVORITE ALBUM WHILE WORKING ON THIS PAGE!)

MAYBE
STRUGGLING
IS A SIGN OF
PROGRESS.

EMOTIONAL BAGGAGE

IMAGINE YOUR LIFE AS A VACATION. WHAT WOULD YOU NEED TO PACK (FIGURATIVELY OR LITERALLY) TO MAKE THE MOST OF YOUR TRIP? IN THE SUITCASE, WRITE EVERYTHING YOU'D BRING.

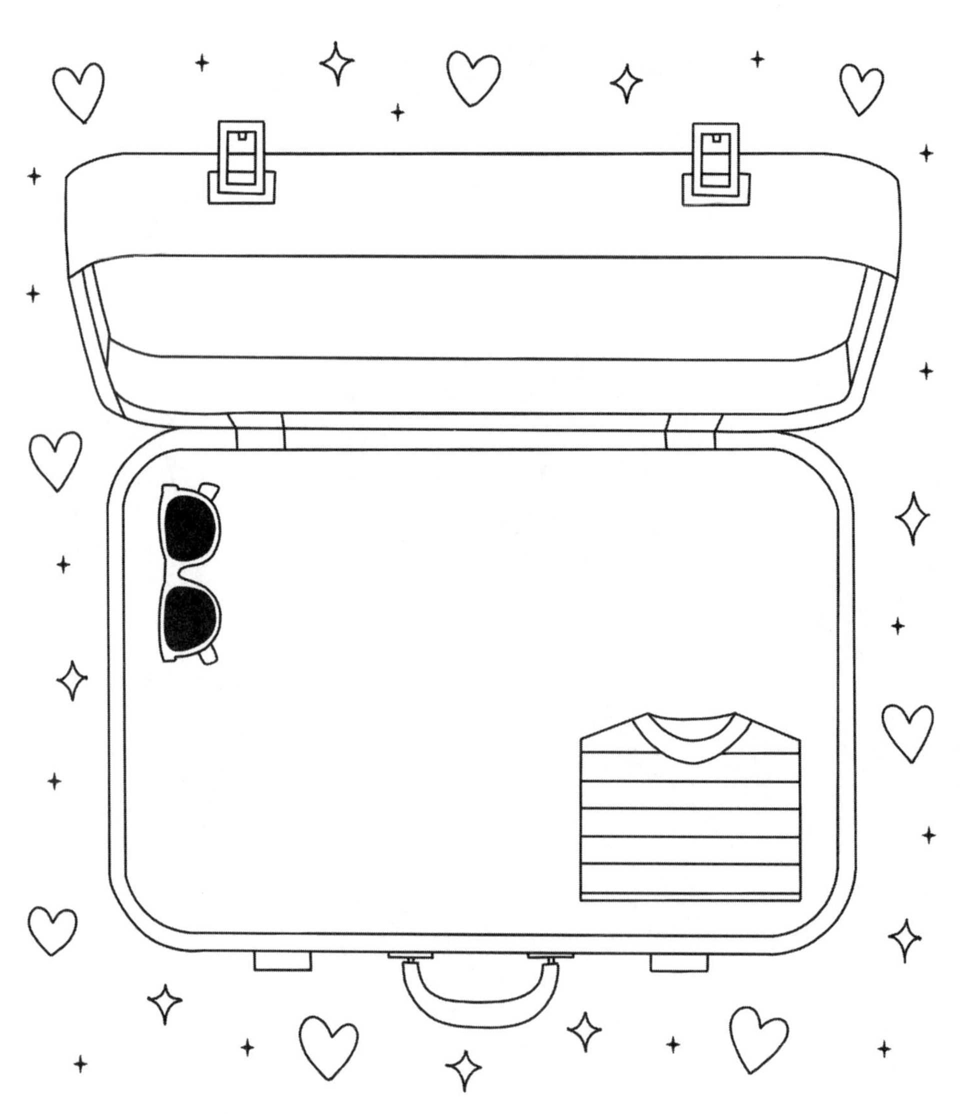

IF YOU WANT
TO SHINE A
LIGHT ON YOUR
FEELINGS, YOU
HAVE TO SIT
WITH THEM.

ONLY ONE OF YOU

CELEBRATE YOUR UNIQUENESS BY WRITING SOME OF YOUR ONE-OF-A-KIND TRAITS ON THE SNOWFLAKES. THESE DON'T HAVE TO BE ANYTHING BIG – ANYTHING THAT MAKES YOU YOU!

IF EVERYTHING FELT GOOD ALL OF THE TIME, NOTHING WOULD EVER FEEL GOOD.

RELEASE YOUR PAST

SOMETIMES IT'S DIFFICULT TO LET GO OF MISTAKES. IF YOU'RE HAVING A HARD TIME RELEASING THEM, WRITE THEM ON THE BALLOONS. COLOR THEM IN AND IMAGINE SETTING THEM FREE.

FREEDOM
COMES FROM
FACING WHAT
YOU FEAR.

CREATIVITY CANVAS

ON THE CANVAS, DRAW SOMETHING THAT REPRESENTS HOW YOUR DAY IS GOING OR HOW YOU'RE FEELING TODAY. (ABSTRACT SCRIBBLES ARE PERFECTLY ACCEPTABLE!)

FOCUS
ON WHAT
YOU WANT,
NOT WHAT
YOU DON'T.

SHAKE THINGS UP

EVERY ONCE IN A WHILE, IT'S A GOOD IDEA TO SWITCH THINGS UP. IN THE SNOW GLOBE, WRITE ABOUT SOMETHING YOU'D LIKE TO CHANGE IN YOUR LIFE – BIG OR SMALL!

ALLOW
OLD CYCLES
TO DIE SO
THAT NEW
ONES CAN
BEGIN.

ALWAYS GROWING

NO MATTER YOUR AGE, YOU'RE ALWAYS GROWING AND CHANGING. ON EACH PETAL, WRITE ABOUT A WAY YOU'VE GROWN OR CHANGED IN RECENT YEARS.

COMPREHENSION
ISN'T REQUIRED
FOR COMPASSION.

SCAVENGER HUNT

PRACTICE PAYING ATTENTION BY LOOKING OUT FOR THE ITEMS ILLUSTRATED BELOW. WHEN YOU FIND THEM – IN REAL LIFE OR ONLINE – COLOR THEM IN UNTIL THE WHOLE PAGE IS FILLED.

YESTERDAY
WHERE YOU ARE NOW IS NOT WHERE YOU WILL ALWAYS BE.
TOMORROW

ALL YOU NEED TO DO

WHAT'S THE ONLY THING YOU NEED TO BE DOING RIGHT NOW?
COLOR IN ALL THE SPACES THAT CONTAIN A DOT IN THE
LETTERS BELOW TO FIND OUT THE ANSWER.

IT'S OKAY TO
OUTGROW THOSE WHO
ARE NO LONGER
GROWING.

MINDSET GALLERY

KNOWING HOW YOU FEEL AND REACT TO YOUR EMOTIONS IS SO IMPORTANT. IN THE FRAMES, WRITE HOW YOU FEEL AND WHAT YOU TYPICALLY DO WHEN YOU EXPERIENCE THAT EMOTION.

DON'T FORGET
TO BE KIND
TO YOURSELF.

MIXED FEELINGS

SOMETIMES FEELINGS AREN'T ALWAYS CLEAR. TO GAIN CLARITY, WRITE ABOUT SOMETHING (OR SOMEONE) YOU HAVE MIXED FEELINGS ABOUT ON THE PAINT CAN BELOW.

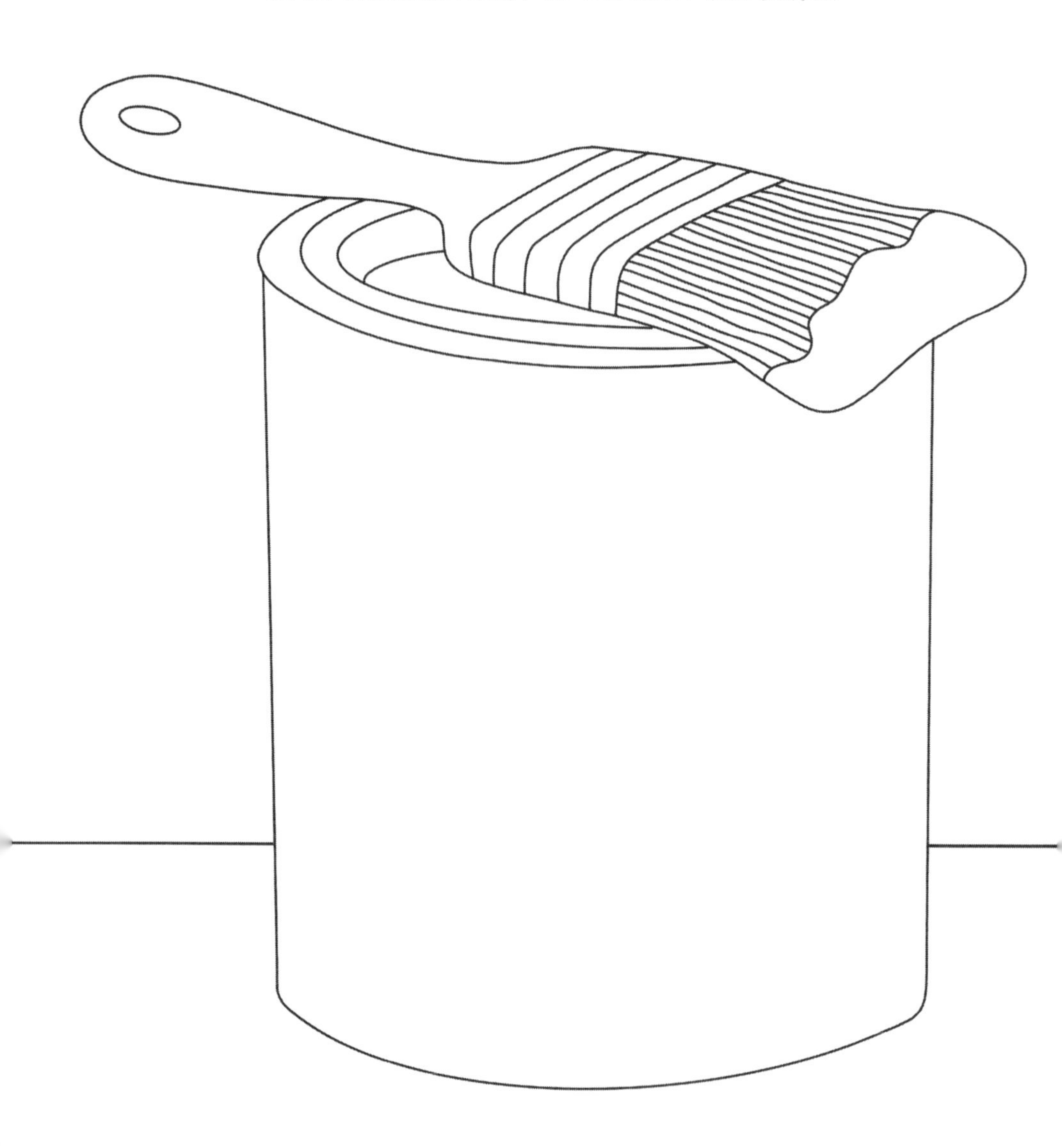

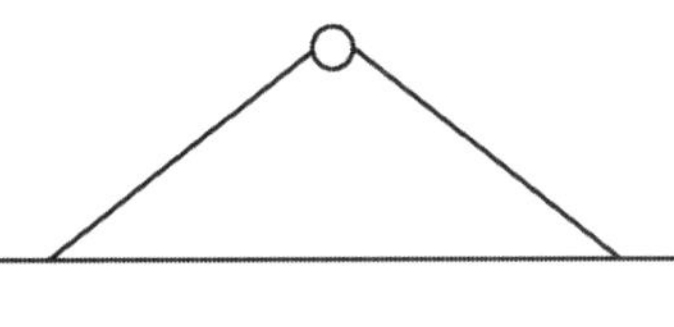

JUST BECAUSE SOMETHING
ISN'T HAPPENING RIGHT NOW
DOESN'T MEAN IT NEVER WILL.

MON	TUE	WED	THR	FRI	SAT	SUN
			1	2	3	4
5	6	7	8	9	10	11
12	13	14	15	16	17	18
19	20	21	22	23	24	25
26	27	28	29	30	31	

RECALL YOUR JOY

TAKE TIME TO CELEBRATE AND REMEMBER THE GOOD TIMES.
ON THE PHOTOS BELOW, WRITE ABOUT (OR DRAW!)
SOME OF YOUR FAVORITE JOYFUL MEMORIES.

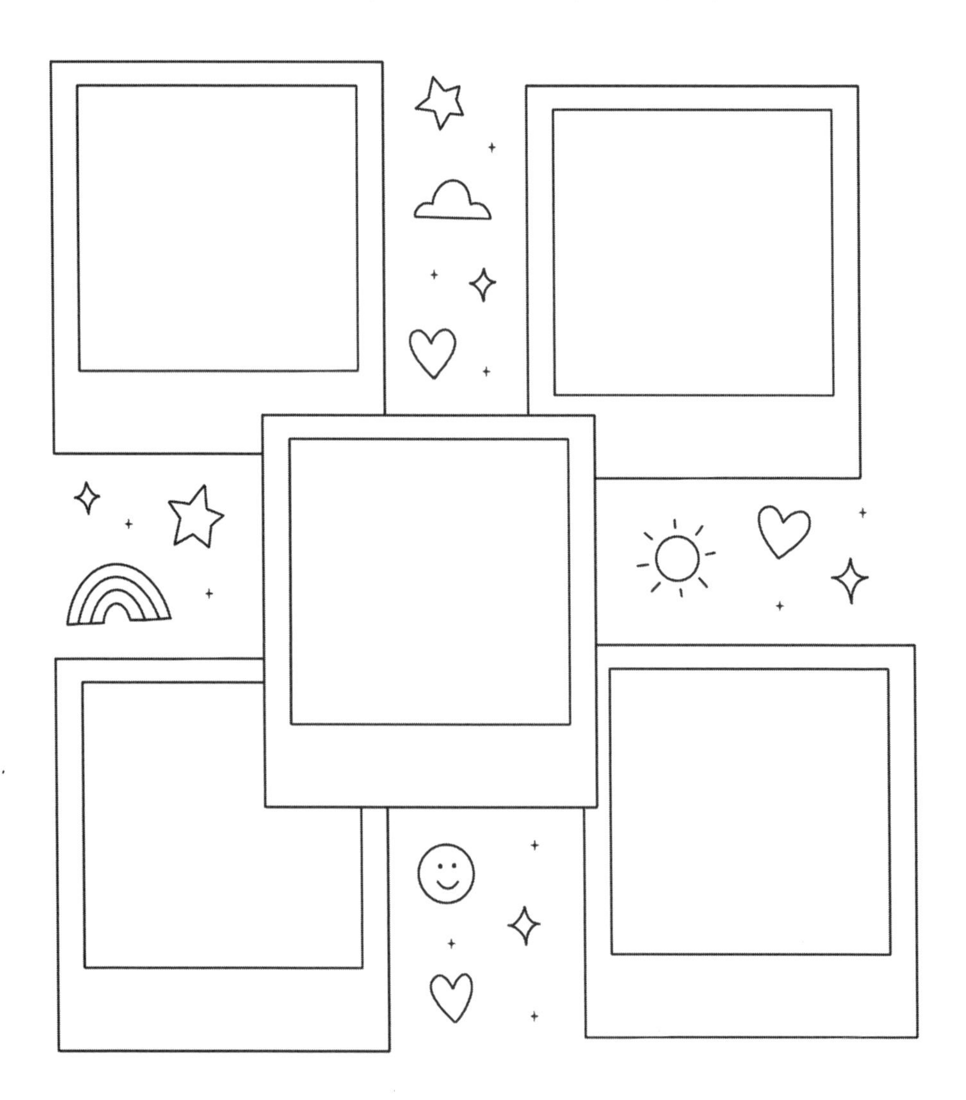

DON'T SETTLE FOR SCRAPS
WHEN YOU DESERVE A MEAL.

RECIPE FOR CALM

AS YOU COLOR IN EACH OF THE INGREDIENTS, LABEL THEM WITH THINGS THAT HELP YOU KEEP CALM, SUCH AS "SUPPORT," "ALONE TIME," "SOOTHING MUSIC," "A GOOD FRIEND," ETC.

WHAT YOU
TELL YOUR
MIND TO LOOK
FOR IS WHAT
IT'LL FIND.

CELEBRATE YOURSELF

ON EACH CAKE SLICE, WRITE ABOUT SOMETHING YOU'VE ACCOMPLISHED. IT CAN BE AS SMALL AS GETTING OUT OF BED TODAY OR AS BIG AS REACHING A LIFELONG GOAL.

OPTIMISM ISN'T
STANDING IN THE RAIN
AND SAYING, "IT'S NOT
RAINING." IT'S TRYING TO
FIND A SILVER LINING
IN THE CLOUDS.

MINE FOR THE GOOD

IT'S EASY TO FOCUS ON WHAT'S NOT WORKING, BUT LET'S SHIFT THE FOCUS TO WHAT'S GOING WELL. ON EACH GEMSTONE, WRITE DOWN THINGS THAT ARE WORKING OUT RIGHT NOW.

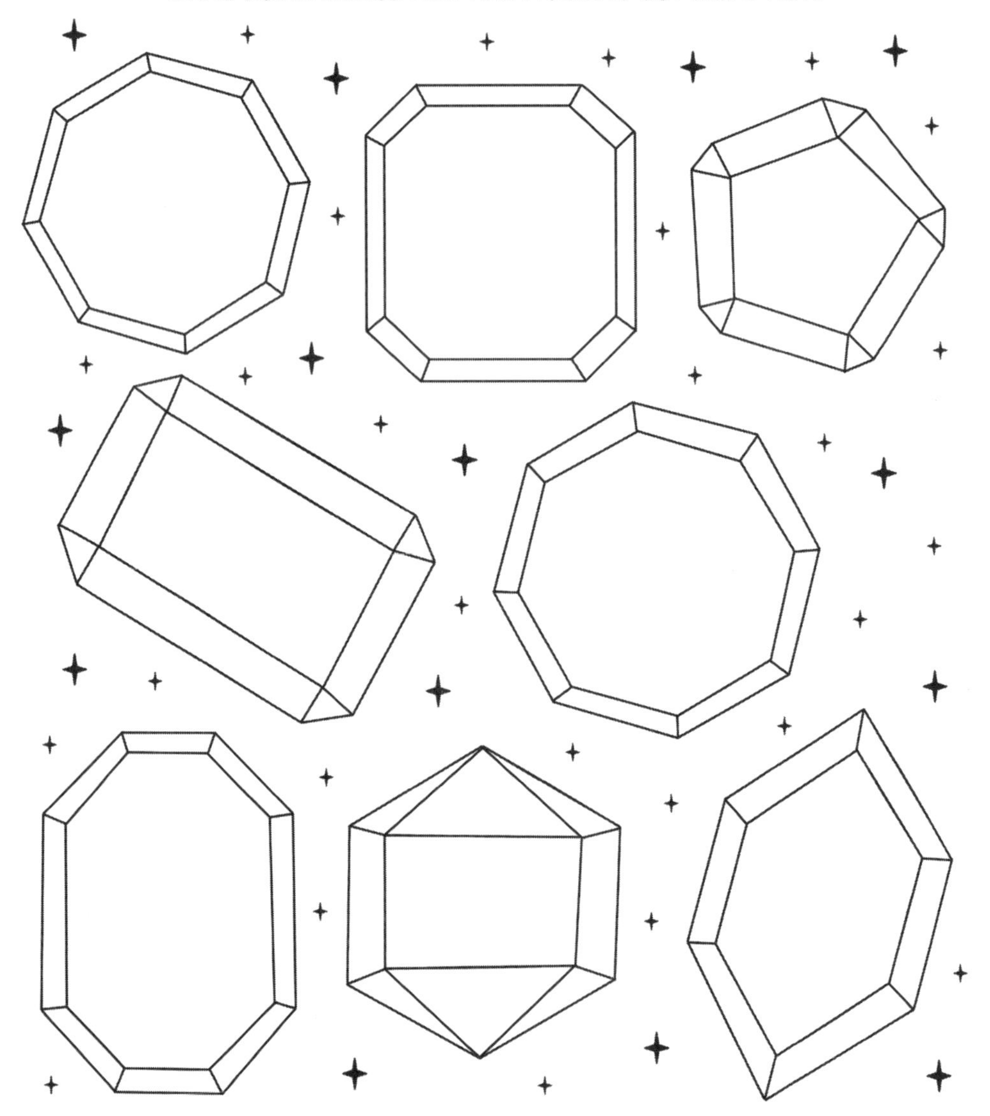

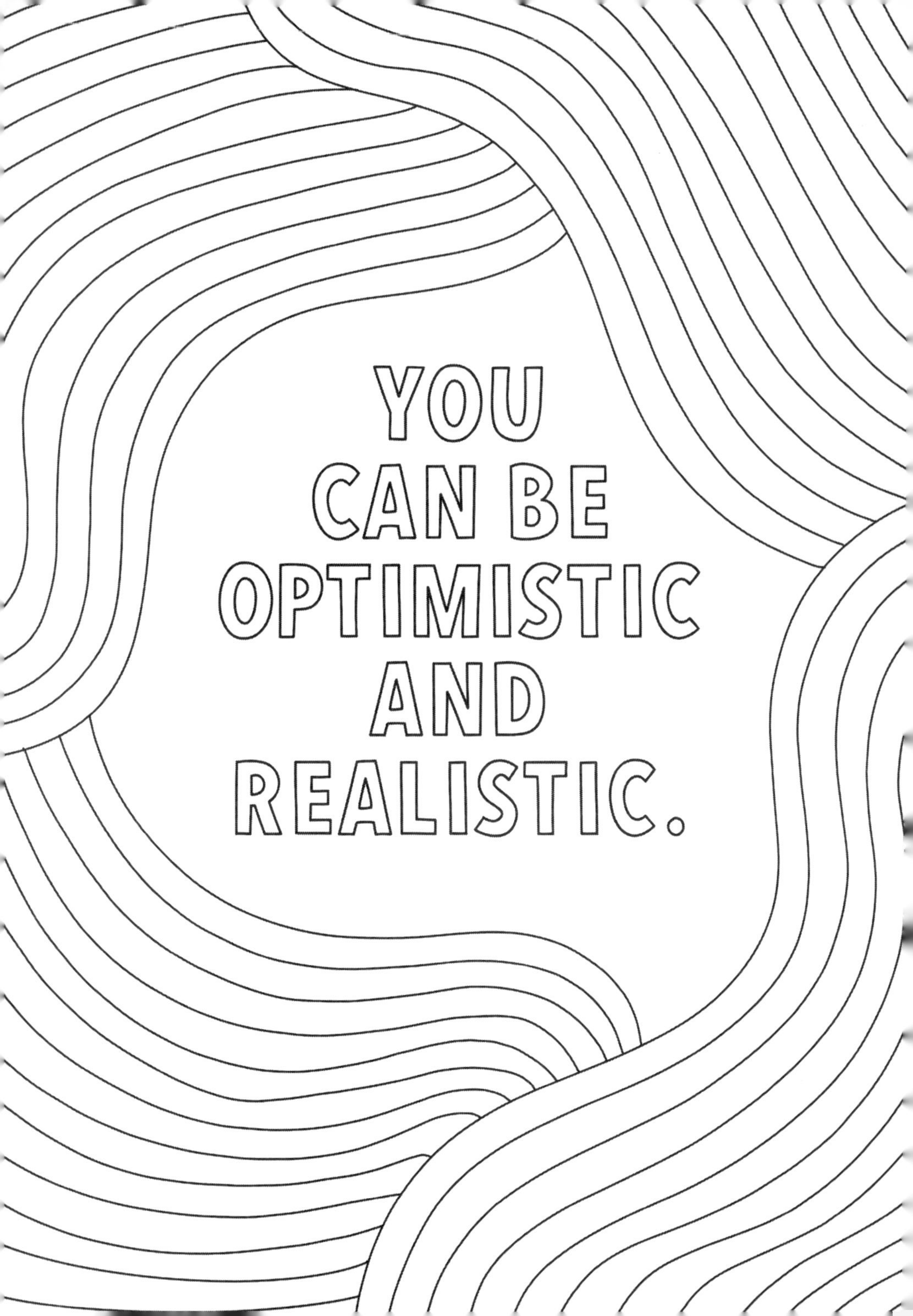
YOU
CAN BE
OPTIMISTIC
AND
REALISTIC.

ACTION IS MAGIC

ABOVE THE CAULDRON, WRITE DOWN A GOAL YOU'D LIKE TO TACKLE. THEN, IN THE CAULDRON, LIST FIVE ACTIONS YOU CAN TAKE TO MOVE TOWARD THAT GOAL. TRY TO DO ONE TODAY!

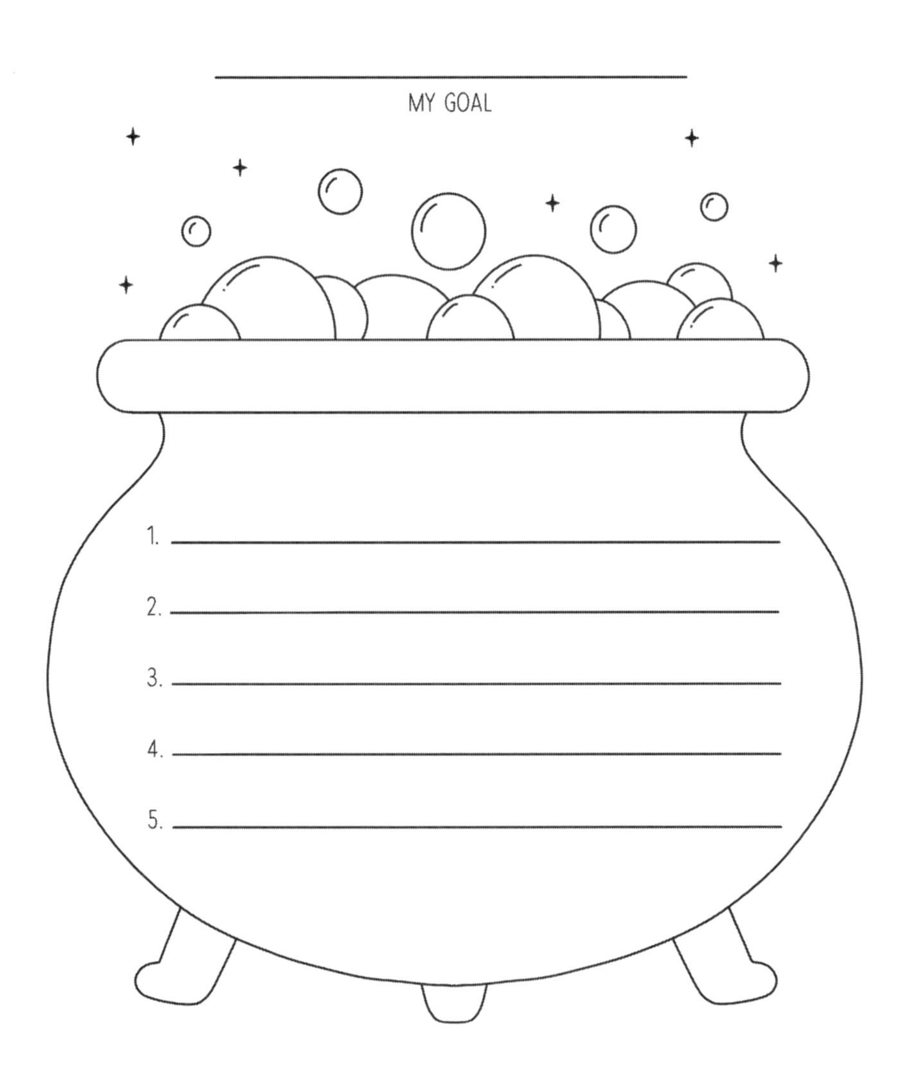

SOME THINGS
ARE DESTINED
TO EVOLVE.
LET THEM.
SOME THINGS
ARE DESTINED
TO DISSOLVE.
LET THEM.

FIND THE RAINBOW

COLOR IN THE RAINBOW BELOW IN ORDER (RED, ORANGE, YELLOW, GREEN, BLUE, INDIGO, VIOLET). AFTER COLORING EACH SECTION, LOOK AROUND THE ROOM FOR THINGS IN THAT COLOR. THIS WILL HELP YOU FOCUS ON THE PRESENT MOMENT.

PAY ATTENTION TO
THE MOMENTS THAT
MAKE YOU FORGET
THE CLOCK IS
TICKING.

DEFINE YOURSELF

WRITE YOUR NAME VERTICALLY IN THE BOX BELOW. THEN WRITE AN ADJECTIVE OR PHRASE YOU'D USE TO DESCRIBE YOURSELF STARTING WITH EACH LETTER IN YOUR NAME.

DON'T FORGET TO CHECK
IN WITH YOURSELF AND
MAKE SURE YOU STILL WANT
THE THINGS YOU ALWAYS
THOUGHT YOU WANTED.

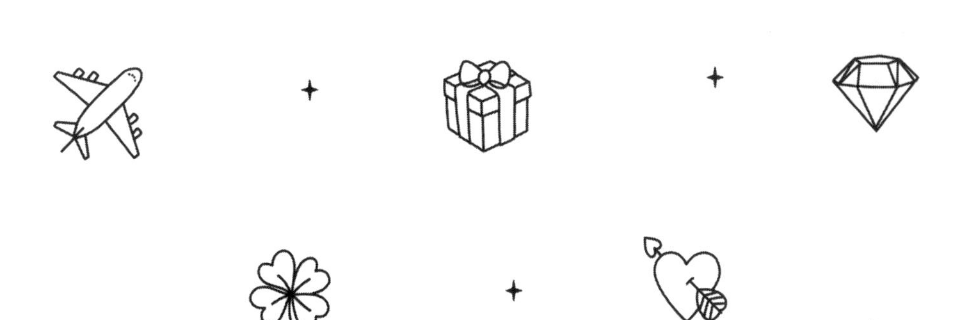

CREATED CONNECTIONS

ON THE QUILT'S SQUARES, WRITE THE NAMES OF PEOPLE WHO HAVE POSITIVELY IMPACTED YOUR LIFE. AS YOU COLOR THE SQUARES, REFLECT ON HOW THEY'VE INFLUENCED YOU.

YOU WERE
NOT PUT
ON THIS
EARTH TO
SPEND
ALL OF
YOUR TIME
WORRYING.

WHAT IF...?

WHEN WE'RE WORRIED, OUR "WHAT-IFS" TEND TO SKEW NEGATIVE. BUT YOU CAN FLIP THAT AROUND AND DO MORE POSITIVE PONDERING BY ANSWERING THE QUESTIONS BELOW.

WHAT IF EVERYTHING YOU'RE WORRIED ABOUT WORKS OUT FOR THE BEST? HOW WILL IT LOOK IF ALL OF IT TURNS OUT OKAY?

WHAT IF EVERYTHING IN YOUR LIFE STARTS GETTING BETTER AND BETTER? HOW WILL IT FEEL IF THAT HAPPENS?

WHAT IF THE BEST DAYS OF YOUR LIFE ARE YET TO COME? WHAT WOULD THESE FUTURE DAYS LOOK LIKE?

IT'S OKAY IF
YOU'RE STILL
TRYING TO
FIGURE OUT
WHAT'S GOOD
FOR YOU.

FILL YOUR CUPS

ON THE TEACUPS, LIST AS MANY POSITIVES AS YOU CAN ABOUT WHAT'S HAPPENING IN THE PRESENT MOMENT.

STAY CLOSE TO WHAT AND
WHO FEELS LIKE HOME.

FIND WHAT YOU SEEK

YOUR MIND WILL SHOW YOU WHAT YOU LOOK FOR. COLOR IN THE OBJECTS BELOW, CHOOSE YOUR FAVORITE, AND LOOK FOR IT OVER THE NEXT FEW DAYS. NOTICE HOW MANY TIMES YOU SEE IT IN REAL LIFE AND ONLINE. CONSIDER HOW YOU CAN APPLY THIS "FIND WHAT YOU SEEK" IDEA TO BIG-PICTURE CONCEPTS LIKE OPTIMISM, LOVE, SUCCESS, ETC.

FOCUS ON
WHAT'S GOING
WELL RIGHT
NOW.

OPEN YOUR MIND

BELOW ARE SOME QUESTIONS TO OPEN YOUR MIND. WRITE YOUR ANSWERS IN THE BOXES. THEN SHARE THE QUESTIONS WITH FRIENDS FOR MORE INSIGHTS.

HOW DO YOU VERIFY WHETHER A THOUGHT IS TRUE?

IS THERE ANYTHING YOU DON'T WANT TO ADMIT TO YOURSELF?

WHAT ASPECTS OF LIFE SEEM TO COME MOST EASILY TO YOU?

DO YOU WANT EXTERNAL ENCOURAGEMENT OR INTERNAL INSPIRATION?

IS MEANING CREATED FOR YOU, OR DO YOU CREATE IT YOURSELF?

WHAT WOULD THE DICTIONARY DEFINITION OF YOU LOOK LIKE?

DO YOU TEND TO FOLLOW YOUR HEART OR YOUR HEAD?

IS HAPPINESS OR THE PURSUIT OF IT MORE IMPORTANT TO YOU?

DISCARD ANY
IDEAS OF HOW
YOUR HEALING
"SHOULD" LOOK.

ABC'S OF SELF-CARE

CHOOSE ONE OF THESE SELF-CARE IDEAS TO DO TODAY, AND COLOR IN THE LETTER AFTER YOU'VE DONE IT. RETURN TO THIS PAGE WHENEVER YOU NEED SELF-CARE INSPIRATION.

A ASK FOR HELP	B BREATHWORK	C CREATE ART	D DIGITAL DETOX
E ESCAPE ROUTINE	F FIX A MEAL	G GET GRATEFUL	H HYDRATE
I INSPIRE OTHERS	J JOURNAL	K KEEP BEING KIND	L LAUGH
M MAKE A PLAN	N NOTICE NATURE	O ORGANIZE	P PLAY MUSIC
Q QUIET TIME	R READ A BOOK	S SLEEP	T TELL A STORY
U UNPLUG	V VISUALIZE JOY	W WATCH A SUNRISE	X (E)XERCISE
	Y (TRY) YOGA	Z ZONE OUT	

SEEK OUT
OPPORTUNITIES
TO EXPERIENCE
MOMENTS
OF JOY.

DEFINE PRODUCTIVITY

YOU GET TO DECIDE WHAT A "PRODUCTIVE" DAY LOOKS LIKE, AND IT DOESN'T NEED TO HAVE A THING TO DO WITH GETTING A LOT OF WORK DONE! WRITE YOUR OWN DEFINITION BELOW.

MY DEFINITION OF A PRODUCTIVE DAY:

EVEN IN TIMES OF DARKNESS,
THERE IS A LIGHT IN YOU.

IF YOU FEEL ANXIOUS

THE QUESTIONS BELOW CAN HELP WHEN YOU'RE FEELING ANXIOUS. AS YOU COLOR IN THE ILLUSTRATION, ASK YOURSELF THESE QUESTIONS. COME BACK ANY TIME YOU FEEL ANXIOUS!

IS THIS THOUGHT ABSOLUTELY 100% TRUE?

IS IT HELPFUL TO THINK ABOUT THIS?

DO I NEED TO THINK ABOUT IT RIGHT NOW?

IS THIS THOUGHT ADDING VALUE TO MY LIFE?

HOW DOES IT FEEL TO THINK ABOUT IT?

IS THIS AN OLD OR A NEW THOUGHT?

DID I THINK THIS THOUGHT ON MY OWN?

IF NOT, WHERE DID THIS IDEA COME FROM?

IS THIS THOUGHT PART OF A PATTERN?

HOW ELSE MIGHT I THINK OF THIS IDEA?

WHAT'LL HAPPEN IF I LET THIS THOUGHT GO?

AM I LETTING THIS THOUGHT DEFINE ME?

IS THIS IDEA CREATING PEACE OR PAIN?

CAN I SHARE THIS THOUGHT WITH OTHERS?

WHO WOULD I BE WITHOUT THIS THOUGHT?

IS THIS THOUGHT DISTORTING MY REALITY?

AM I LEARNING ANYTHING FROM THIS THOUGHT?

NOT EVERY EMOTION HAS AN EASY EXPLANATION.

(AND THAT'S OKAY!)

THE SHAPE OF CALM

COLORING CAN HELP YOU KEEP CALM. ASSIGN A COLOR TO EACH OF THE NUMBERS BELOW, THEN USE THOSE HUES TO COLOR IN THE SHAPES AND CREATE SOME CALM.

1. = ________ 2. = ________ 3. = ________

4. = ________ 5. = ________

KEEP
LOOKING
FOR BEAUTY
AROUND
EVERY BEND.

LET YOUR MIND WANDER

BELOW ARE QUESTIONS MEANT TO INSPIRE MIND-WANDERING. WRITE YOUR ANSWERS IN THE CLOUDS OR COLOR IN THE CLOUDS AS YOU THINK THROUGH YOUR ANSWERS.

HOW WOULD YOU LIVE DIFFERENTLY IF YOU COULD READ OTHERS' MINDS?

WHAT WOULD YOU FIND IF YOU OPENED A DOOR TO ANOTHER WORLD?

WHICH MAGICAL PLACE OR CREATURE DO YOU WISH EXISTED IN REALITY?

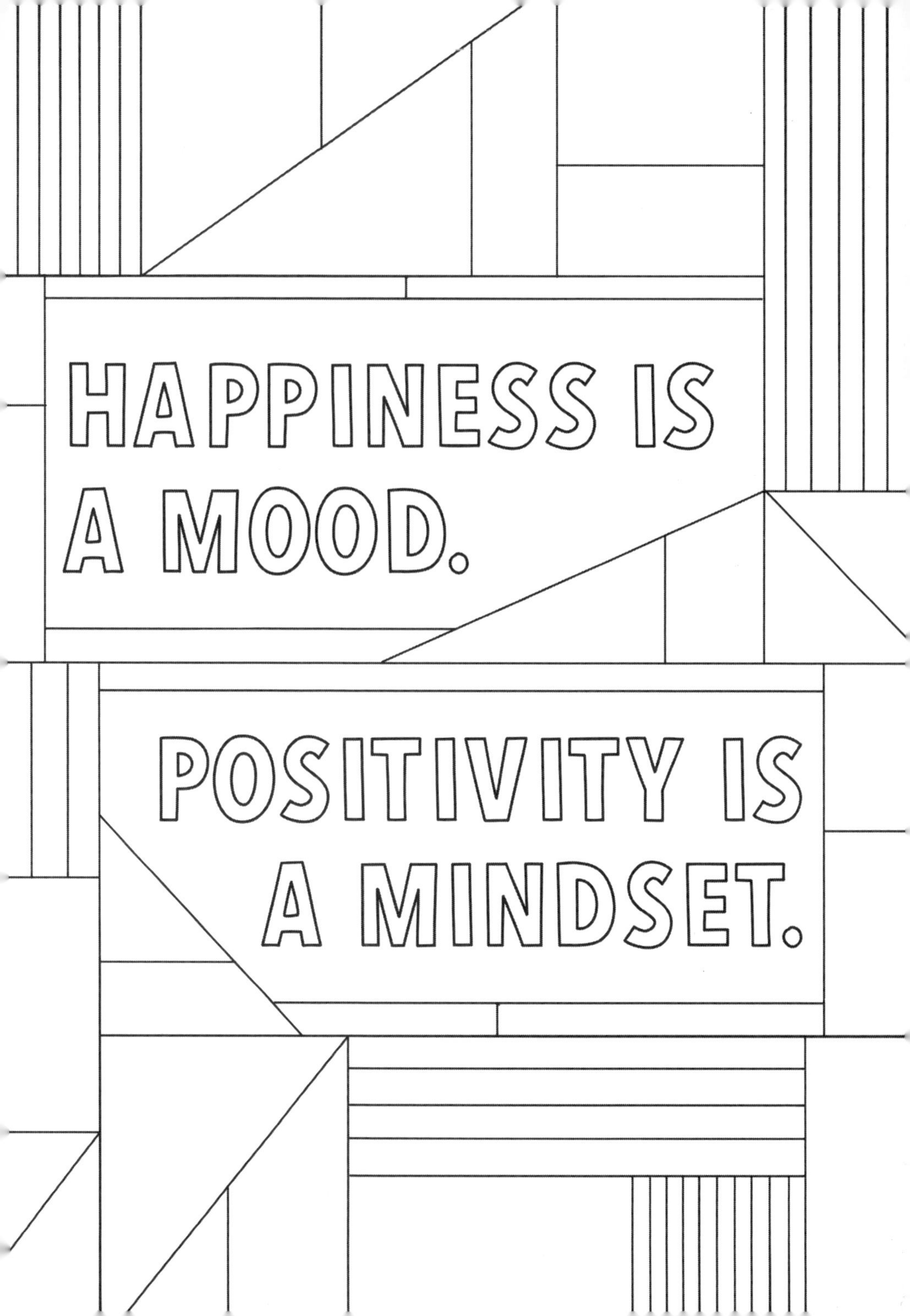
HAPPINESS IS
A MOOD.
POSITIVITY IS
A MINDSET.

MINDFUL MIRRORING

BRING YOURSELF BACK TO THE PRESENT MOMENT
BY USING WHAT YOU SEE IN THE LEFT SIDE OF EACH BOX
TO COMPLETE THE DRAWING IN THE RIGHT SIDE.

NOTICE HOW THINGS
ACTUALLY FEEL.
NOT HOW YOU THINK
THEY SHOULD.
NOT HOW YOU WISH
THEY WOULD.

MEET YOUR FEELINGS

IN EACH SEGMENT OF THE WHEEL, DRAW AN ILLUSTRATION OR CHARACTER DEPICTING HOW THAT EMOTION FEELS. IF YOU'D RATHER NOT DRAW, WRITE ABOUT HOW IT FEELS IN YOUR BODY.

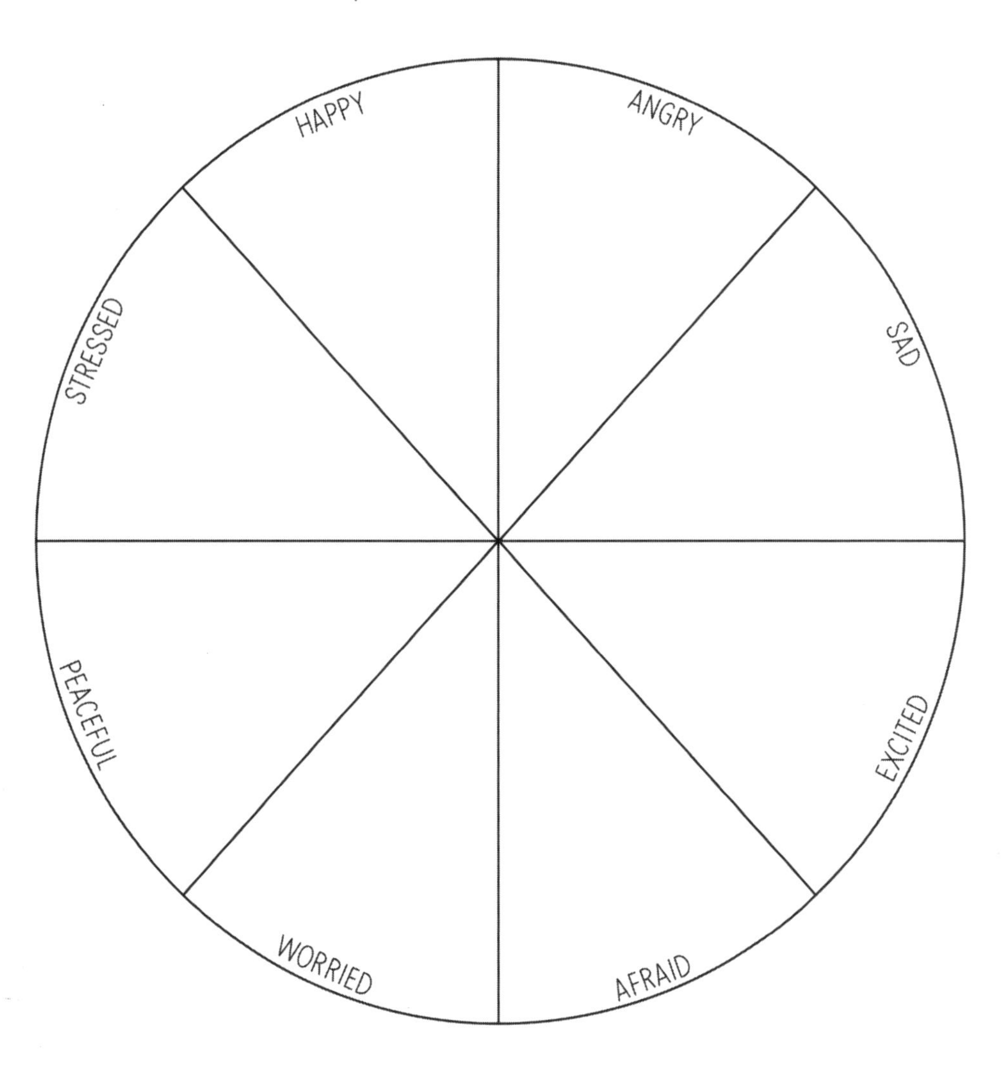

SEASONS
CHANGE AND SO
WILL YOU. KEEP
GROWING.

GRAFFITI WALL

ABOVE THE BRICKS, SCRIBBLE YOUR FEELINGS AS IF YOU'RE WRITING GRAFFITI ON A BLANK WALL. DRAW DOODLES, TAG YOUR EMOTIONS, ETC. UNTIL THE WALL IS FILLED.

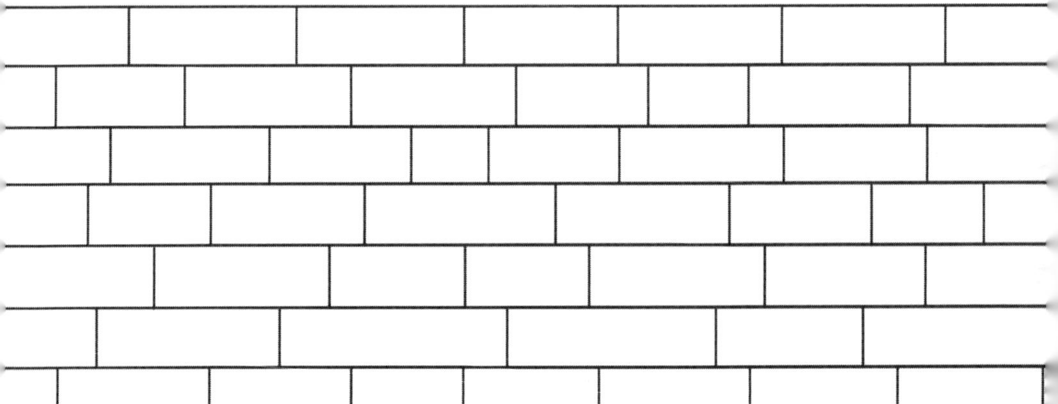

YOU ARE
ALLOWED
TO REST.

SEEK SWEETNESS

TO REMIND YOU OF LIFE'S SWEETNESS, WRITE A LITTLE THING THAT BRINGS YOU JOY UNDER EACH OF THE SWEETS BELOW. THE SMALLER AND MORE MUNDANE, THE BETTER!

START
YOU DON'T HAVE TO PLAY THE GAME OF LIFE THE SAME WAY EVERYONE ELSE DOES. YOU CAN MAKE UP YOUR OWN RULES.

LET-IT-GO LIST

MOST OF US HAVE A FEW THINGS WE'D BE BETTER OFF NOT HAVING IN OUR LIVES. TAKE A LOOK AT THE LIST BELOW AND CHECK OFF WHAT YOU'D LIKE TO WORK ON RELEASING.

- ☐ WORRYING ABOUT WHAT IS OUT OF YOUR CONTROL
- ☐ EXPECTATIONS FOR HOW THINGS "SHOULD" BE
- ☐ UNHEALTHY RELATIONSHIPS THAT BRING YOU PAIN
- ☐ THE DESIRE TO CONTROL EVERYTHING IN YOUR LIFE
- ☐ UNPRODUCTIVE HABITS THAT HOLD YOU BACK
- ☐ SELF-LIMITING BELIEFS THAT LEAD TO SELF-DOUBT
- ☐ THE FEAR OF LEAVING YOUR COMFORT ZONE
- ☐ COMPARING YOUR LIFE TO THE LIVES OF OTHERS
- ☐ THE REFUSAL TO TAKE A CHANCE ON THE UNKNOWN
- ☐ A BELIEF THAT YOU CAN MAKE EVERYONE HAPPY
- ☐ ACTIVITIES AND HOBBIES YOU DON'T ENJOY
- ☐ GUILT ABOUT SITUATIONS YOU CANNOT CHANGE
- ☐ THE IDEA OF A "PERFECT" VERSION OF YOURSELF

NEVER LOSE
YOUR SENSE
OF
WONDER

GET OUT OF YOUR MIND

TO GET OUT OF YOUR HEAD AND BACK INTO THE MOMENT, CHOOSE AN ACTIVITY BELOW. AFTER YOU COMPLETE IT, COLOR IT IN. KEEP GOING UNTIL THE WHOLE PAGE IS COLORED IN.

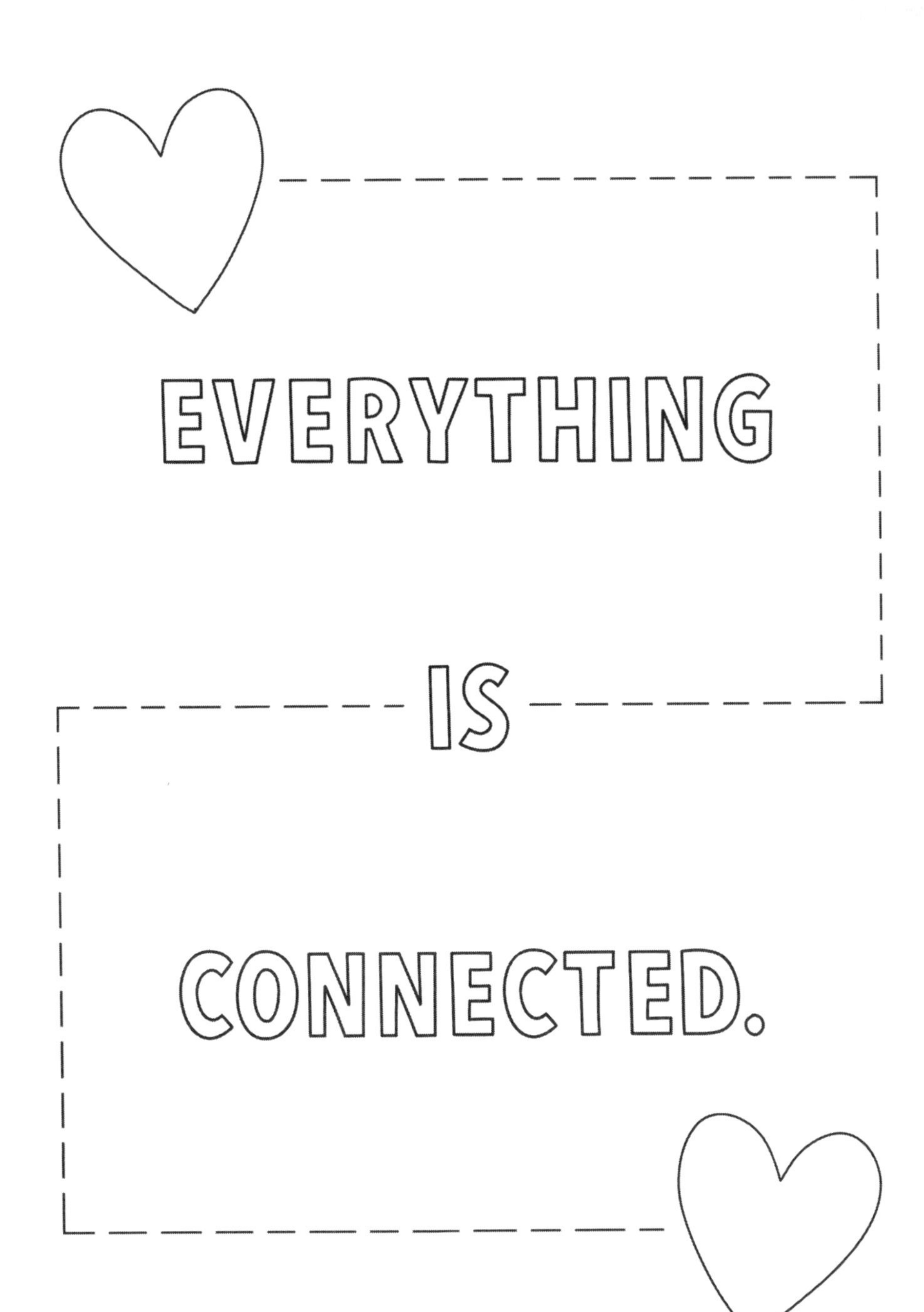
EVERYTHING
IS
CONNECTED.

LESSONS LEARNED

WE'RE ALWAYS LEARNING, AND IT CAN HELP TO BE REMINDED OF THE KNOWLEDGE WE'VE ACQUIRED. ON EACH OF THE SUPPLIES BELOW, WRITE ONE LIFE LESSON YOU'VE LEARNED.

THE ONLY WAY TO BE TRULY FREE
IS TO LET THE PAST AND FUTURE BE.

TAKE FIVE

SET A TIMER FOR FIVE MINUTES AND WRITE ANYTHING THAT COMES TO YOUR MIND – HOW YOU'RE FEELING, A GROCERY LIST, RANDOM IDEAS, ETC. – ON THE LINES BELOW.

TODAY WILL NEVER COME AGAIN. BE KIND. PROTECT YOUR PEACE. APPRECIATE EVERYTHING. SAY WHAT YOU MUST. DO NOT WAIT. GIVE BACK. LOVE. AND LOVE SOME MORE.

KINDS OF COMFORT

ON THE LEFT IS A LIST OF THINGS THAT MIGHT BRING COMFORT.
ON THE RIGHT IS SPACE TO ADD YOUR OWN COMFORTS.
BOOKMARK THIS PAGE AND COME BACK ON DIFFICULT DAYS.

	MY COMFORTS LIST
REREADING A BELOVED BOOK	______________
INHALING A LOVELY, FAMILIAR SCENT	______________
SNUGGLING INTO A COZY BED	______________
RETURNING HOME AFTER BEING AWAY	______________
HUGGING SOMEONE YOU LOVE	______________
FOCUSING ON THE PRESENT MOMENT	______________
ENJOYING YOUR FAVORITE MEAL	______________
WATCHING FILMS FROM CHILDHOOD	______________
PULLING ON A SOFT, OLD T-SHIRT	______________
SOAKING IN A HOT BUBBLE BATH	______________
LISTENING TO YOUR FAVORITE SONG	______________
RECALLING A HAPPY MEMORY	______________
HEARING JOY IN A FRIEND'S LAUGH	______________
TRUSTING IT'LL ALL WORK OUT	______________

IF YOU'RE LOST,
I HOPE YOU FIND THE PATH.

IF YOU'RE GRIEVING,
I HOPE YOU FIND COMFORT.

IF YOU'RE STUCK,
I HOPE YOU FIND INSPIRATION.

IF YOU'RE ALONE,
I HOPE YOU FIND CONNECTION.

IF YOU'RE IN THE DARK,
I HOPE YOU FIND YOUR LIGHT.

SEASONAL SENSATIONS

CHECK IN WITH YOUR SENSES BY DRAWING (OR WRITING) WHAT YOU LIKE ABOUT EACH SEASON BELOW. PAY SPECIAL ATTENTION TO YOUR LEAST FAVORITE SEASON!

SPRING	SUMMER
WINTER	AUTUMN

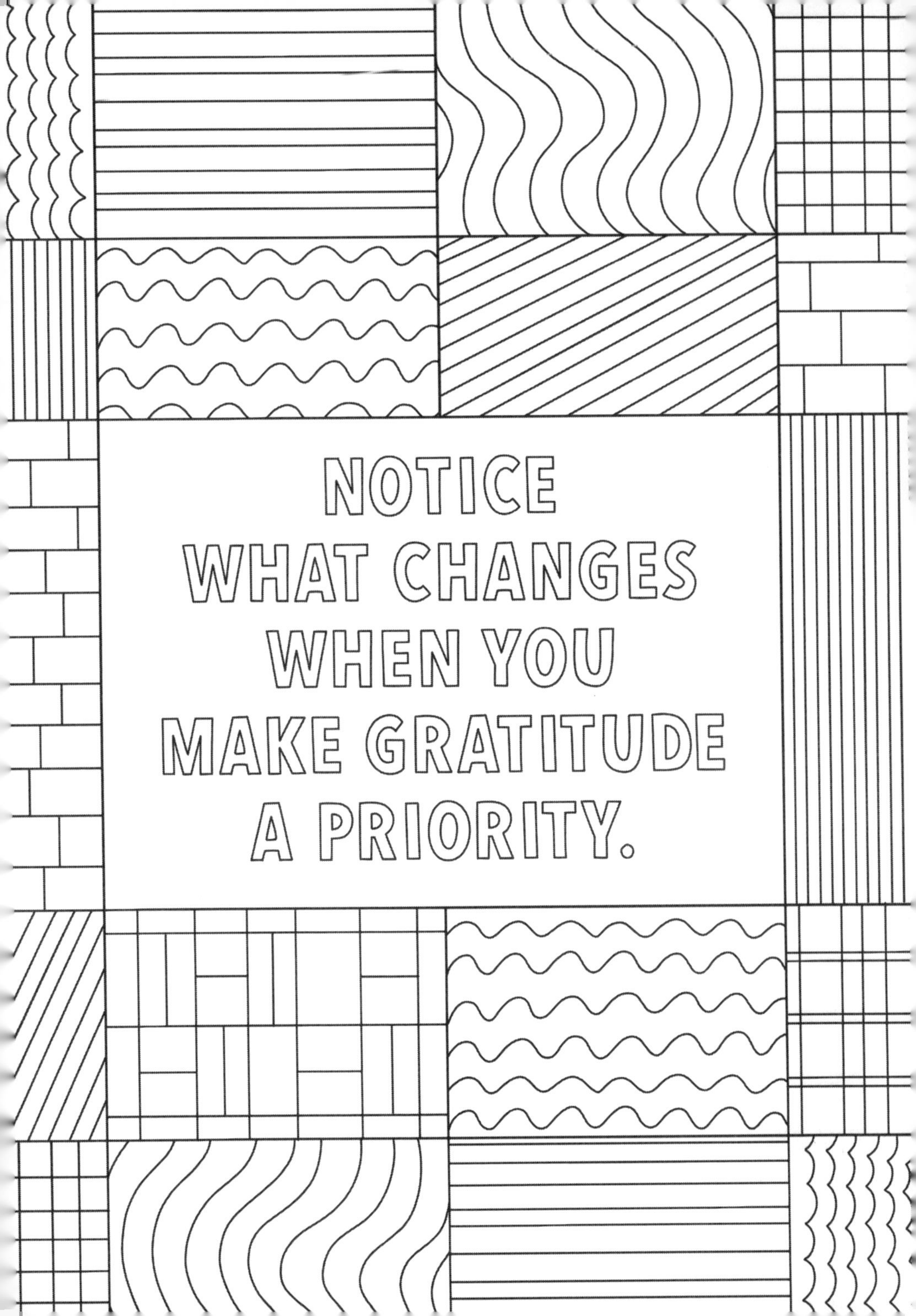
NOTICE
WHAT CHANGES
WHEN YOU
MAKE GRATITUDE
A PRIORITY.

CHOOSE YOUR CARD

PICK THE CARD THAT RESONATES MOST WITH YOU TODAY AND COLOR IT IN. COME BACK TO THIS PAGE TO COLOR IN THE REST OF THE CARDS WHEN YOU NEED THEIR MESSAGES.

YOU WON'T MISS
OUT ON WHAT'S
MEANT FOR YOU.
KEEP GOING.

REASON REFLECTION

ON THE LINES BELOW, WRITE DOWN HOW YOU FEEL ABOUT THIS QUOTE: "EVERYTHING HAPPENS FOR A REASON." DO YOU THINK IT'S TRUE? WHY OR WHY NOT?

BEING
A HUMAN
BEING
IS HARD.
BE
KIND TO
YOURSELF.

TIME TO TRACE

TRACE THE DOTTED LINES BELOW. THIS MAY SEEM LIKE A SIMPLE ACTIVITY, BUT IT CREATES A BODY-MIND CONNECTION THAT WILL BRING YOU BACK TO THE PRESENT MOMENT.

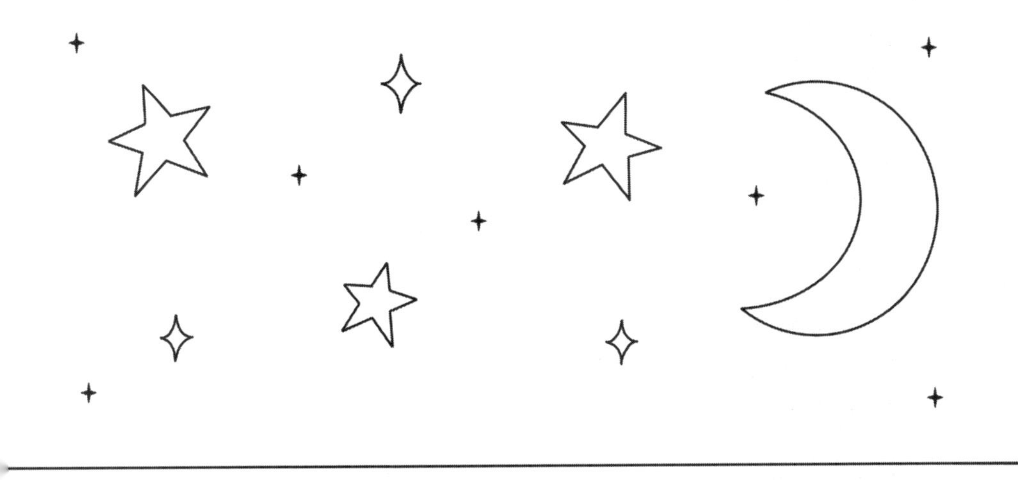

YOU ARE MORE
THAN WHO YOU
WERE. YOU CAN
START OVER
ANYTIME.

TODAY'S TO-DO LIST

LIST EVERYTHING YOU'D LIKE TO DO TODAY, BUT NOTHING CAN BE RELATED TO WORK OR PRODUCTIVITY. SOME IDEAS TO GET YOU STARTED: MAKE SOMEONE LAUGH, HAVE A DANCE PARTY, TRY A NEW FOOD, GO OUTSIDE TO ENJOY NATURE, ETC.

- [ ] ______________________________
- [ ] ______________________________
- [ ] ______________________________
- [ ] ______________________________
- [ ] ______________________________
- [ ] ______________________________
- [ ] ______________________________
- [ ] ______________________________
- [ ] ______________________________
- [ ] ______________________________
- [ ] ______________________________

YOU ARE A WORK IN PROGRESS, NOT A PROBLEM TO BE SOLVED.

MULTIPLE CHOICE

TAKE A BREAK FROM WHATEVER YOU'VE BEEN THINKING ABOUT AND ANSWER THE QUESTIONS BELOW. (DON'T THINK TOO HARD ABOUT YOUR ANSWERS – GO WITH YOUR FIRST INSTINCT!)

MY HEART FEELS LIKE:

(A) A KALEIDOSCOPE
(B) THE NIGHT SKY
(C) A SOOTHING SONG
(D) AN OPEN ROAD

TRUE COMFORT IS:

(A) A PERSON I LOVE
(B) KNOWLEDGE
(C) TIME SPENT ALONE
(D) A COZY BED

THIS MOMENT IS:

(A) LIKE A SUNSET
(B) MORE THAN IT WAS
(C) A WILD PARTY
(D) THE WHOLE POINT

IT'S TIME FOR ME TO:

(A) FIND A NEW PATH
(B) WISH ON A STAR
(C) TRUST THE PROCESS
(D) PLAN MY ESCAPE

A BROKEN HEART:

(A) IS A MUSEUM
(B) CHANGES EVERYTHING
(C) LEADS TO HOPE
(D) WILL ALWAYS HEAL

I CAN'T WAIT TO:

(A) SEE THEM AGAIN
(B) LAUGH LOUDLY
(C) HEAR THE RAIN
(D) FEEL LIKE ME

THE BEST GIFT IS:

(A) HANDMADE
(B) GIVEN, NOT RECEIVED
(C) BEING ALIVE
(D) NOT AN OBJECT

SOMEDAY I WILL:

(A) ACCEPT WHAT IS
(B) REINVENT MYSELF
(C) FIND TRUE LOVE
(D) SEEK SIMPLICITY

I WOULD STAR IN:

(A) A COMEDY
(B) A ROMANCE
(C) A MYSTERY
(D) A THRILLER

MY IDEAL WORLD HAS:

(A) ALL MY FRIENDS
(B) NO WORKDAYS
(C) LOVE FOR EVERYONE
(D) A NEW REALITY

REMEMBER TO ASK:

(A) WHY YOU'RE HERE
(B) WHO MATTERS MOST
(C) HOW IT BEGAN
(D) WHEN TO LEAVE

MY MIND FEELS LIKE:

(A) A DARK CAVE
(B) THE UNIVERSE
(C) A ROUGH SKETCH
(D) MY TRUE SELF

YOU ARE THE
CURATOR OF YOUR
OWN WISDOM.

HARD-DAY HELPERS

IF YOU'RE HAVING A HARD DAY, HERE ARE POSITIVE ACTIVITIES YOU CAN TRY TO MAKE THE DAY A LITTLE EASIER. COLOR THEM IN AS YOU DO THEM – OR JUST COLOR IN THE WHOLE PAGE!

FOCUS ON WHAT
YOU HAVE, NOT ON
WHAT YOU LACK.

CLAP FOR OTHERS

IT FEELS GOOD TO CELEBRATE AND COMPLIMENT OTHERS. IN THE SPEECH BUBBLES, WRITE ABOUT OTHERS' SUCCESSES AND/OR GOOD TRAITS. (THEN TELL THEM, IF YOU LIKE!)

SOMETIMES
YOU HAVE TO
PACK UP THE
PAST IN ORDER
TO MAKE ROOM
FOR THE FUTURE.

CONNECT THE DOTS

CONNECT THE DOTS BELOW. WHEN YOU'RE DONE, CONNECT DOTS 1 AND 23. THEN COLOR IN THE IMAGE WITH COLORS NOT TYPICALLY USED FOR THIS KIND OF OBJECT.

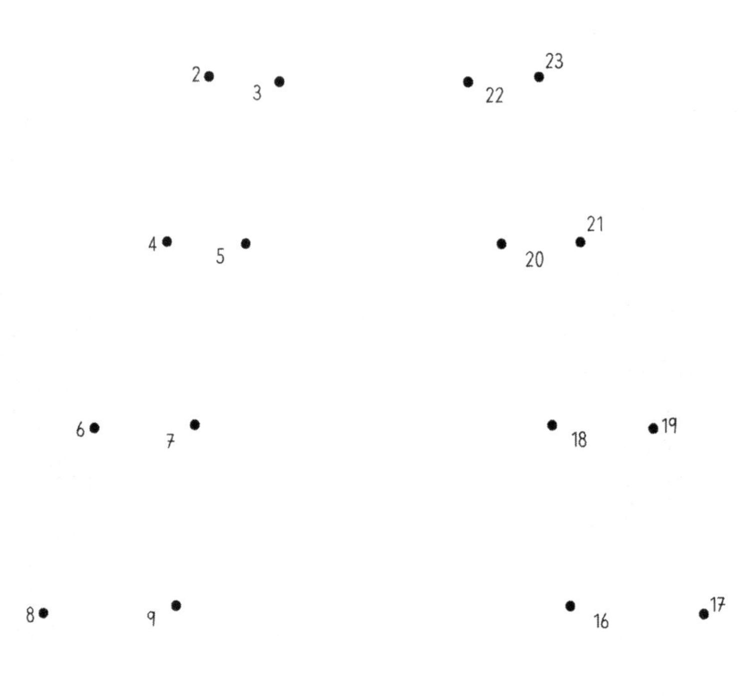

MAYBE WHAT'S AROUND
THE NEXT CORNER IS
WONDERFUL. KEEP GOING.
KEEP GOING

NOTE TO (FUTURE) SELF

WRITE ABOUT SOMETHING THAT'S BOTHERING YOU RIGHT NOW. SET A REMINDER TO COME BACK TO THIS PAGE SO YOUR FUTURE SELF CAN SEE HOW IT ENDED UP WORKING OUT.

TODAY'S DATE: ______________________________

DON'T LET
"WHAT IF"
GET IN THE
WAY OF
WHAT IS.

THE IDEAL DAY

IN THE WINDOW, WRITE ABOUT (OR DRAW!) YOUR IDEAL DAY – THE WEATHER, ACTIVITIES YOU'D DO, PEOPLE YOU'D SEE, ETC.

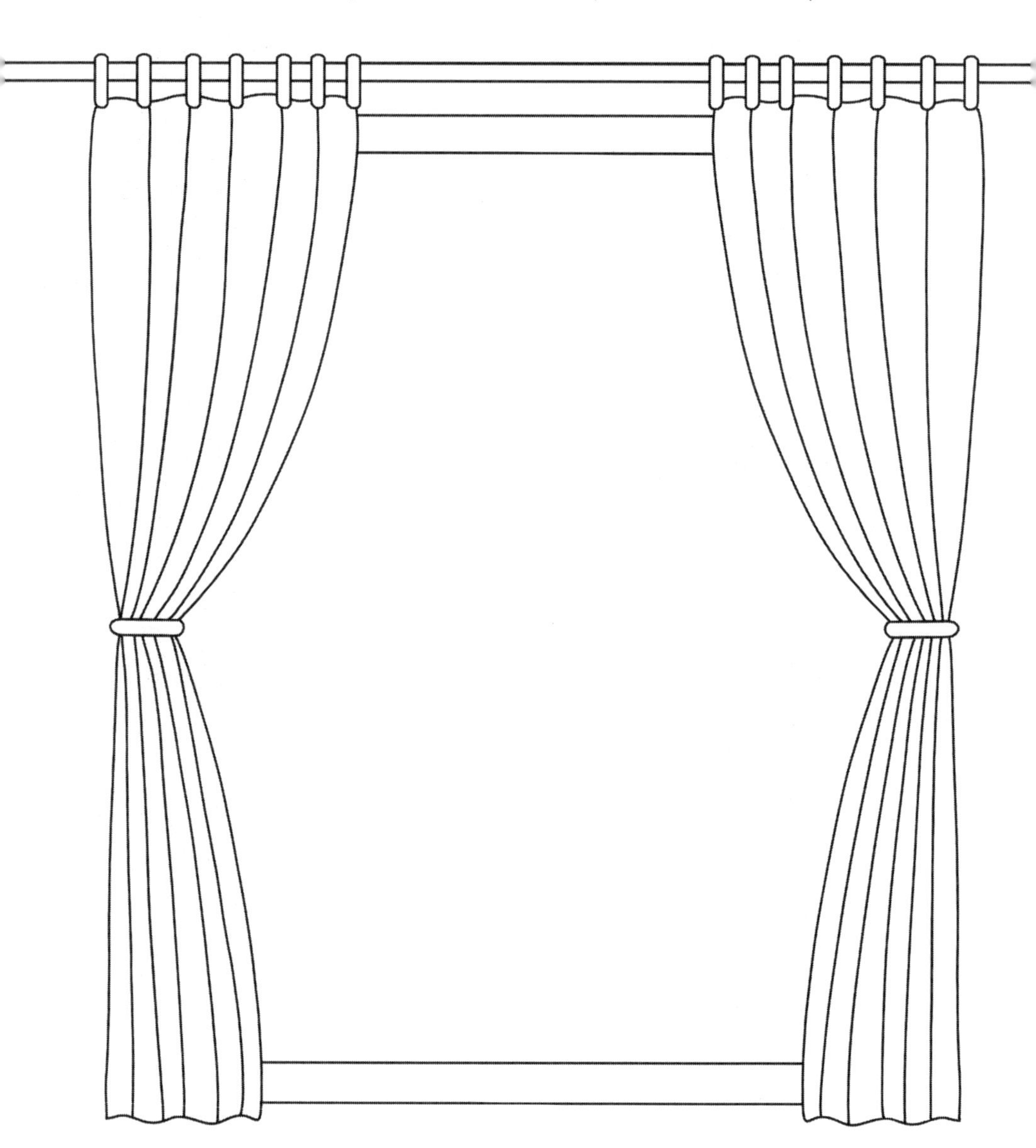

EVERYONE HAS A CHAPTER THEY DON'T WANT TO READ ALOUD.

HEY, IT'S OKAY

THE SHAPES BELOW ARE FILLED WITH THINGS IT'S PERFECTLY NORMAL TO EXPERIENCE. COLOR IN THE ONES THAT RESONATE, AND FILL IN THE BLANK SHAPES WITH SOME OF YOUR OWN.

FEELINGS AREN'T FACTS.

(BUT THEY ARE USEFUL GUIDES.)

SURVIVE THE STORM

WHAT ARE SOME ACTIVITIES THAT HAVE MADE YOUR BAD DAYS BETTER? WRITE THEM ON THE CLOUDS, AND USE THIS PAGE AS A GUIDE THE NEXT TIME YOU'RE HAVING A DOWN DAY.

BEING
PRODUCTIVE
ISN'T LIFE'S
PURPOSE.

FILL IN THE BLANKS

FILL IN THE LINES BELOW WITH YOUR ANSWERS. (TRY TO WRITE WHAT COMES TO MIND RIGHT AWAY WITHOUT THINKING TOO MUCH!) BONUS: ASK A FRIEND HOW THEY'D ANSWER.

SOMETIMES ______________________ IS THE BRAVE THING.

TIME TURNS ______________ TO ______________.

YOU'VE GOT NO REASON TO BE ______________________.

IF YOU NEVER ___________, YOU'RE NEVER GOING TO ___________.

THE BEST PEOPLE IN LIFE ARE ______________________.

I KNEW ______________________ WHEN I WAS YOUNG.

YOU ARE WHAT YOU ______________________.

I THINK I AM FINALLY ______________________.

I ONCE WAS ______________, BUT NOW I AM ______________.

NEVER BE SO ______________ THAT YOU FORGET TO ______________.

LONG STORY SHORT, I ______________________.

PUTTING SOMEONE FIRST ONLY WORKS WHEN ______________.

I WANT TO BE DEFINED BY WHAT I ______________________.

LET THIS
MOMENT BE
WHAT IT IS.

YOUR WORDS MATTER

THE WAY WE SPEAK TO OURSELVES GREATLY IMPACTS OUR LIVES. AS YOU COLOR IN EACH OF THE SPEECH BUBBLES, SAY EACH OF THE AFFIRMATIONS TO YOURSELF.

I AM ALWAYS LEARNING.

I TREAT MYSELF LIKE A FRIEND.

I AM DOING THE BEST I CAN.

I TRUST MY INTUITION.

I AM ALLOWED TO CHANGE.

I AM STRONGER THAN I WAS.

I APPRECIATE WHO I AM.

I CAN RELEASE CONTROL.

I CAN FACE CHALLENGES.

I AM WORTHY OF KINDNESS.

I AM PROUD OF MY HARD WORK.

I DESERVE GOOD THINGS.

I AM MAKING PROGRESS.

YOU ARE
WORTHY OF ALL
THE LOVE AND
AFFECTION THAT
YOU SHOW TO
OTHERS.

FORGIVE YOUR MISTAKES

SOMETIMES WE FORGET TO FORGIVE OURSELVES THE WAY WE FORGIVE OTHERS. WRITE DOWN ANY MISTAKES YOU'VE MADE (BIG OR SMALL!). THEN CHECK EACH ONE OFF, IMAGINING THE CHECKS AS CONFIRMATIONS OF SELF-FORGIVENESS.

- [ ] ______________________________
- [ ] ______________________________
- [ ] ______________________________
- [ ] ______________________________
- [ ] ______________________________
- [ ] ______________________________
- [ ] ______________________________
- [ ] ______________________________
- [ ] ______________________________
- [ ] ______________________________
- [ ] ______________________________

YOU HAVE SURVIVED EVERYTHING UP UNTIL NOW.
BE PROUD OF YOUR PROGRESS.

A CLOSER LOOK

AS YOU COLOR IN THE IMAGE BELOW, LOOK FOR THE ITEMS FROM THE LIST. BOTH COLORING AND SEARCHING WILL BRING YOUR ATTENTION TO THE MOMENT.

AN ITEM THAT'S TYPICALLY YELLOW

OBJECTS WITH ROUNDED SHAPES

RAINBOWS (OR RAINBOW-COLORED ITEMS)

SOMETHING YOU DON'T SEE OFTEN

ANYTHING YOU MIGHT FIND IN NATURE

ITEMS YOU'D ONLY SEE AT NIGHT

SOMETHING RELATED TO A HOLIDAY

THINGS YOU WOULD FIND AT A SCHOOL

AN ITEM SYMBOLIZING GOOD LUCK

SOMETHING THAT YOU'D LIKE TO EAT

OBJECTS THAT HAVE SHARP EDGES

ITEMS THAT YOU MIGHT WEAR

SOMETHING THAT'S IN YOUR HOUSE

PICK
PEOPLE
WHO PICK
YOU.

SMALLEST JOYS

WRITE DOWN THE SMALLEST, MOST MUNDANE JOYS YOU EXPERIENCE TODAY. ANYTHING THAT MAKES YOUR LIFE A LITTLE BRIGHTER OR EASIER, LIKE TAKING A SIP OF YOUR FAVORITE DRINK OR SEEING THE SUN SHINE THROUGH THE WINDOW.

IT'S OKAY IF
THINGS DON'T
MAKE SENSE
SOMETIMES.
DRINK

MOOD MIXTAPE

FILL OUT THE MOOD-RELATED MUSIC LIST BELOW. THEN MAKE A PLAYLIST OF THESE SONGS SO YOU CAN TURN THEM ON WHEN THE VARIOUS SITUATIONS OR MOODS ARISE.

BEST SONG TO LISTEN TO ON A ROAD TRIP ____________________

BEST SONG TO PUT YOU IN A GOOD MOOD ____________________

BEST SONG WITH A SEASONAL THEME ____________________

BEST SONG TO LISTEN TO WHEN FEELING SAD ____________________

BEST SONG FROM THE DECADE YOU WERE BORN ____________________

BEST SONG TO WAKE UP TO ____________________

BEST SONG SOMEONE ELSE TOLD YOU ABOUT ____________________

BEST SONG TO TURN UP WHEN YOU'RE ANGRY ____________________

BEST SONG FROM A FILM OR TV SHOW ____________________

BEST SONG TO HAVE A DANCE PARTY TO ____________________

BEST SONG WITH RELATABLE LYRICS ____________________

BEST SONG TO LISTEN TO WHEN YOU'RE HAPPY ____________________

BEST SONG TO FALL ASLEEP LISTENING TO ____________________

BEST SONG FOR BOOSTING YOUR ENERGY ____________________

BEST SONG TO RECALL A HAPPY MEMORY ____________________

BEST SONG FOR COPING WITH A BREAKUP ____________________

BEST SONG WITH EMPOWERING LYRICS ____________________

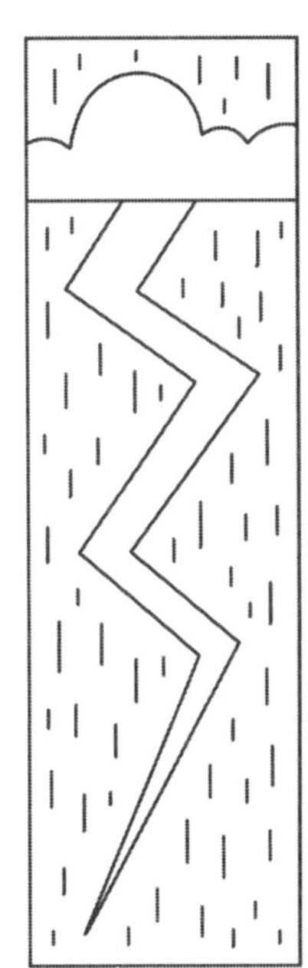

REMINDER:
NO FEELING
IS FOREVER.

MIND THIS MOMENT

BRING YOURSELF BACK TO THE NOW BY TAKING THE TIME TO ANSWER THE MINDFULNESS PROMPTS BELOW.

LIST 3 THINGS YOU CAN SEE THAT ARE ROUND OR THAT CONTAIN CIRCLES.

LIST 3 BEAUTIFUL THINGS YOU CAN SEE.

LIST 3 THINGS YOU CAN SEE THAT HAVE AN INTERESTING TEXTURE OR PATTERN.

LIST 3 THINGS YOU CAN SEE THAT HAVE BLUE ON THEM.

SOMETIMES IT'S A
LONG COMMUTE
FROM ONE FEELING
TO THE NEXT.

MYSTERY PICTURE

USE THE CHART BELOW TO COLOR IN THE GRID AND REVEAL AN INSPIRING IMAGE. LET THIS REMIND YOU THAT YOU DON'T ALWAYS SEE THE WHOLE PICTURE RIGHT AWAY.

1																				
2																				
3																				
4																				
5																				
6																				
7																				
8																				
9																				
10																				
11																				
12																				
13																				
14																				
15																				
16																				
17																				
18																				
19																				
20																				
	A	B	C	D	E	F	G	H	I	J	K	L	M	N	O	P	Q	R	S	T

BLUE	A(2-4, 6-8), B(2, 3, 6), C(1, 2), D(1), E(1), F(1, 2, 10, 11), G(1, 2, 9-11), H(1, 2, 9-11), I(1, 2, 9-11), J(1, 9, 10), K(9, 12), L(9), M(1, 9, 10), N(1, 10, 11, 13), O(1, 12-14), P(1, 2), Q(1, 5), R(1, 5, 6), S(1, 2, 5-7), T(1-3, 5, 8, 9)
YELLOW	B(10), C(9), D(7, 8), E(6, 7), F(6), G(5), H(5), I(5), J(5), K(5), L(5), M(5), N(6), O(7), P(7, 8), Q(8-10), R(10, 11), S(12, 13)
PURPLE	E(10), F(9), G(8), H(8), I(8), J(8), K(8), L(8), M(8), N(9), O(10, 11), P(12, 13)
LIGHT BLUE	D(10), E(9), F(8), G(7), H(7), I(7), J(7), K(7), L(7), M(7), N(8), O(9), P(10, 11), Q(12, 13)
PINK	A(9), B(7, 8), C(6), D(5), E(4), F(4), G(3), H(3), I(3), J(3), K(3), L(3), M(3), N(4), O(4), P(5), Q(6), R(7), S(8, 9), T(10, 11)
ORANGE	A(10), B(9), C(7, 8), D(6), E(5), F(5), G(4), H(4), I(4), J(4), K(4), L(4), M(4), N(5), O(5, 6), P(6), Q(7), R(8, 9), S(10, 11), T(12, 13)
GREEN	C(10), D(9, 20), E(8, 20), F(7, 19, 20), G(6, 19, 20), H(6, 18-20), I(6, 17-20), J(6, 17-20), K(6, 16-20), L(6, 16-20), M(6, 16-20), N(7, 15-20), O(8, 15-20), P(9, 14-20), Q(11, 14-20), R(12-20), S(14-20), T(14-20)
LIGHT GREEN	A(11-20), B(11-20), C(11-20), D(11-19), E(11-19), F(12-18), G(12-18), H(12-17), I(12-16), J(12-16), K(13-15), L(13-15), M(13-15), N(14)

OUTSIDE THE LINES

COLOR IN THE ILLUSTRATION, BUT DON'T STAY INSIDE THE LINES. YOU CAN SCRIBBLE ALL OVER IT, COLOR NEATLY BUT CROSS THE LINES – ANYTHING BUT STAYING IN THE LINES!

APPRECIATE
THE VERSION
OF YOURSELF
THAT EXISTS
RIGHT NOW.

ALL THAT YOU ARE

FILL IN THE AREA AROUND THE CIRCLE WITH POSITIVE ADJECTIVES OR PHRASES THAT DESCRIBE YOU. IF YOU NEED IDEAS, SEARCH ONLINE FOR "POSITIVE ADJECTIVES."

OPTIMISM WON'T CHANGE
THE SITUATION...
...BUT IT WILL CHANGE
HOW THE SITUATION FEELS.

POSTCARD TO THE PAST

WRITE A POSTCARD TO YOUR PAST SELF, EXPLAINING WHAT'S CHANGED. ON THE FRONT OF THE POSTCARD, DRAW (OR WRITE ABOUT) YOUR FAVORITE THINGS ABOUT YOUR LIFE NOW.

THE STORIES YOU TELL YOURSELF MATTER.
CHOOSE THE TONE AND THEMES WISELY.

WHICH WEATHER?

BELOW ARE VARIOUS EMOTIONS REPRESENTED BY WEATHER. COLOR IN THE ONES YOU'VE EXPERIENCED WITHIN THE PAST WEEK. AS YOU COLOR, REMIND YOURSELF THAT FEELINGS ARE JUST LIKE THE WEATHER – THEY COME AND THEY GO.

ENERGIZED

UPSET

PASSIONATE

ANXIOUS

CALM

OPTIMISTIC

SAFE

OVERWHELMED

HOPEFUL

BE GRATEFUL

FOR GROWTH.

NO LONGER / NOT YET

IN THE LEFT COLUMN, WRITE ABOUT HOW YOU'VE CHANGED IN THE PAST YEAR. IN THE RIGHT COLUMN, WRITE ABOUT HOW YOU HOPE TO CHANGE IN THE YEAR TO COME.

YOU ARE NO LONGER WHO YOU WERE.	YOU ARE NOT YET WHO YOU WILL BE.

SENTENCE FINISHER

FINISH EACH OF THE SENTENCES HOWEVER YOU WANT. CHOOSE REALISM OR GET AS IMAGINATIVE AND CREATIVE AS YOU'D LIKE.

THE MESSAGE WRITTEN IN THE SKY SAID ______________________________

____.

AT THE BEGINNING OF AUTUMN, HE ______________________________

____.

AN UNEXPECTED NOISE ______________________________

____.

EVERY DAY, THE OLD OAK TREE ______________________________

____.

WHEN SHE TURNED AROUND, ______________________________

____.

THE DOOR OPENED, AND THEY ______________________________

____.

WILDFLOWERS ON THE ROADSIDE ______________________________

____.

AS THE SUN BEGAN TO SET, ______________________________

____.

TWO BIRDS CIRCLED ______________________________

____.

YOUR
ATTENTION
IS VERY
VALUABLE.
NOTICE
WHAT
KEEPS IT.

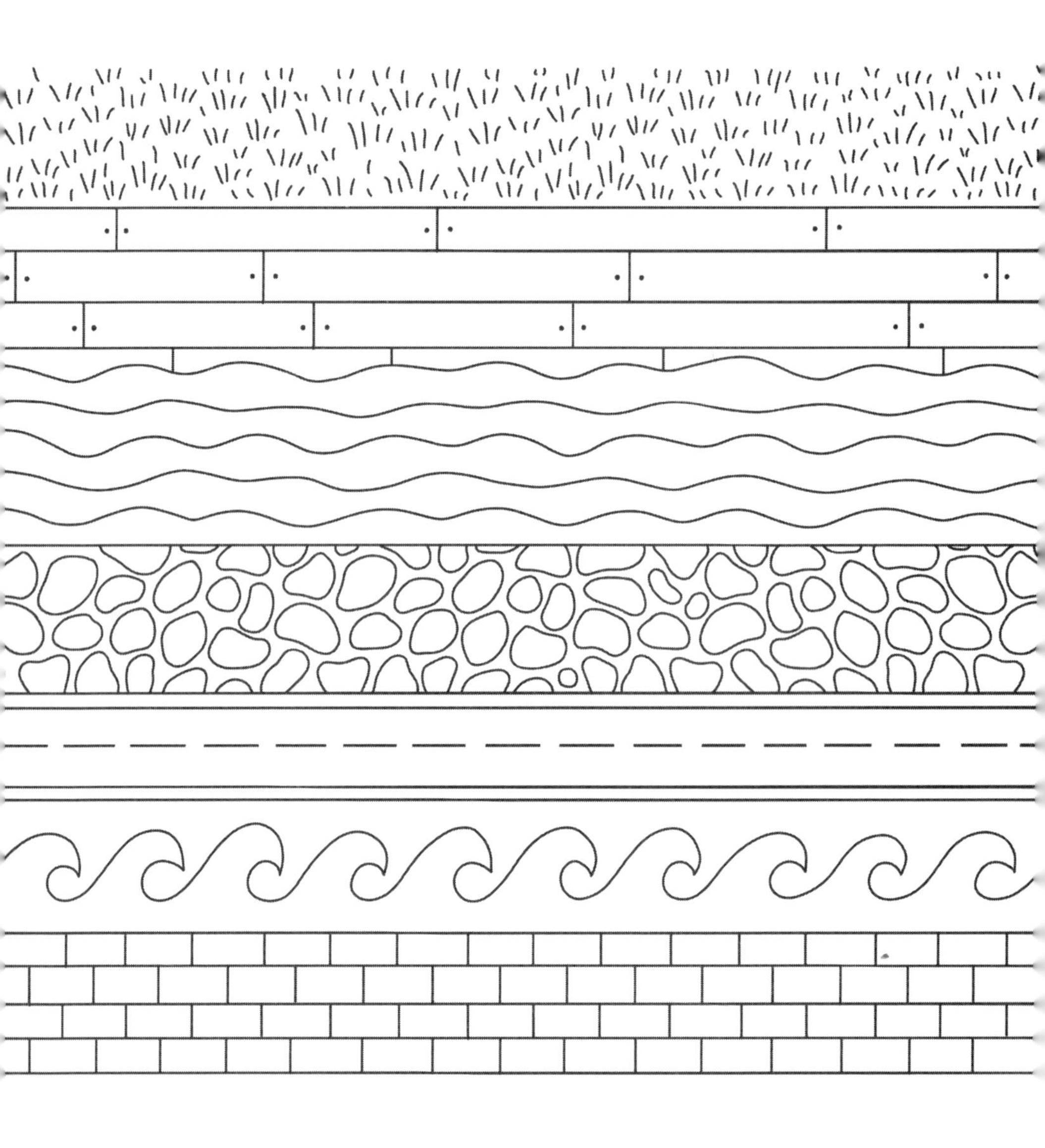

THERE IS NO PATH YOU HAVE TO TAKE.
YOU GET TO MAKE YOUR OWN WAY.

COLOR BY NUMBER

CHOOSE ONE COLOR FOR EACH NUMBER BELOW. MAKE SURE EACH NUMBER HAS A DIFFERENT COLOR. USE THE SUGGESTIONS BELOW AS A GUIDE OR CHOOSE YOUR OWN COLORS.

1. RED OR PINK
2. ORANGE OR YELLOW
3. GREEN OR BLUE
4. INDIGO OR PURPLE
5. PINK OR GREEN
6. YELLOW OR BLUE

HOPE IS A
BRAVE ACT.

PRESENT PAUSE

RETURN TO THE PRESENT MOMENT BY SITTING QUIETLY AND ANSWERING THE QUESTIONS BELOW.

IN THIS MOMENT, I CAN SEE ______________________

____

____

____

IN THIS MOMENT, I CAN HEAR ______________________

____

____

____

IN THIS MOMENT, I CAN TOUCH ______________________

____

____

____

IN THIS MOMENT, I CAN SMELL ______________________

____

____

____

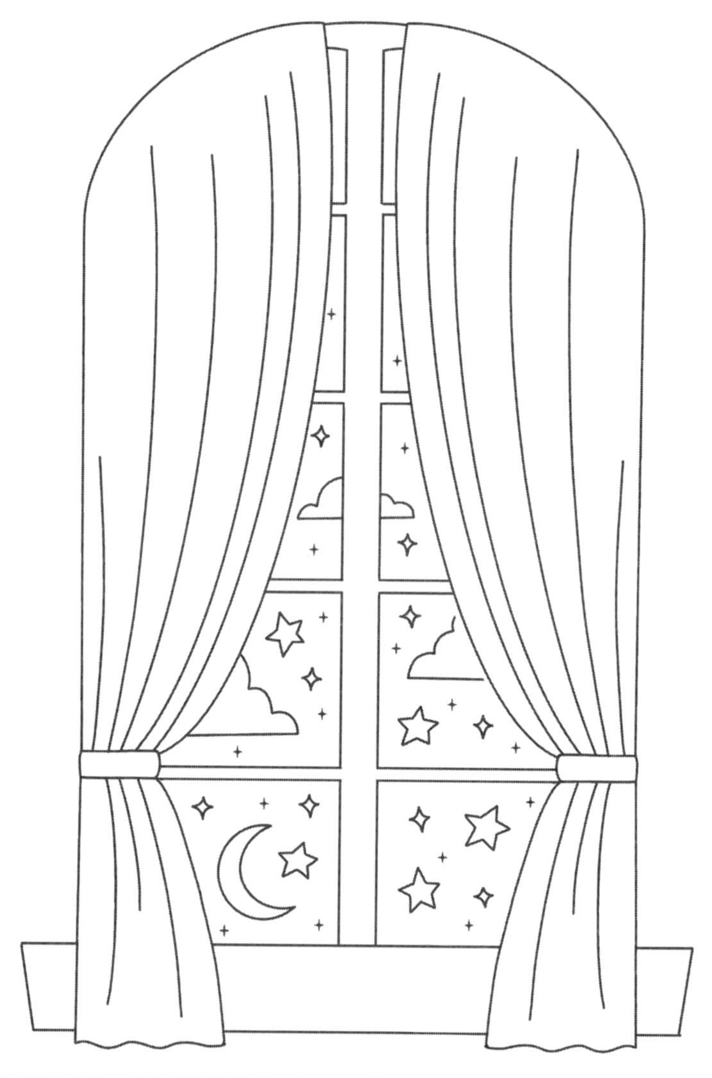

YOUR EXTERNAL CIRCUMSTANCES DON'T NEED TO CHANGE FOR YOUR INTERNAL PERSPECTIVE TO SHIFT.

ALBUM OF NOW

ILLUSTRATE THE ALBUM COVER BELOW WITH A DRAWING OF THE ROOM YOU'RE IN. GO FOR REALISM OR DRAW AN ABSTRACT DESIGN. ADD A TITLE FOR HOW YOU'D SUMMARIZE THE ROOM.

THE ONLY MOMENT YOU HAVE IS NOW. BE HERE.

THE MUST-KNOWS OF ME

IN THE BOXES, LIST WHAT SOMEONE MUST KNOW IF THEY WANT TO UNDERSTAND YOU. THE LIST CAN INCLUDE ANYTHING FROM WHAT YOU EAT FOR BREAKFAST TO YOUR CORE BELIEFS.

IN ORDER TO KNOW ME, YOU MUST KNOW...

IN ORDER TO KNOW ME, YOU MUST KNOW...

IN ORDER TO KNOW ME, YOU MUST KNOW...

IN ORDER TO KNOW ME, YOU MUST KNOW...

IN ORDER TO KNOW ME, YOU MUST KNOW...

IN ORDER TO KNOW ME, YOU MUST KNOW...

COMBAT
ANXIETY
WITH
CREATIVITY.

UNWIND & UNSCRAMBLE

FOCUS YOUR MIND ON UNSCRAMBLING THE WORDS – ALL OF THEM POSITIVE NOUNS OR ADJECTIVES – BELOW.

PIMOMSIT ______________________

NCAEAPTECC ______________________

FMOCROT ______________________

UTPORINOPTY ______________________

AIMOSSNOCP ______________________

EISSNPAPH ______________________

GARCOUE ______________________

IDAUTETGR ______________________

RENEGMETOCANU ______________________

EELUPAFC ______________________

TERIVYITCA ______________________

IMERNPGOEW ______________________

RESNTIYE ______________________

INIIPTRSONA ______________________

IHACYEITNTTU ______________________

ONNDTFICE ______________________

SSEHAUITMN ______________________

ANIRLOXEAT ______________________

BENACNAUD ______________________

NCBEALA ______________________

OPTIMISM, ACCEPTANCE, COMFORT, OPPORTUNITY, COMPASSION, HAPPINESS, COURAGE, GRATITUDE, ENCOURAGEMENT, PEACEFUL, CREATIVITY, EMPOWERING, SERENITY, INSPIRATION, AUTHENTICITY, CONFIDENT, ENTHUSIASM, RELAXATION, ABUNDANCE, BALANCE

GOOD
THINGS
COME FROM
GRATEFUL
THOUGHTS.

EMOTIONAL DECORATOR

IMAGINE THE ROOM BELOW IS REPRESENTATIVE OF HOW YOU FEEL RIGHT NOW. DECORATE IT WITH THE COLORS, PATTERNS, ART, RUGS, VIEW, ETC. THAT ILLUSTRATE YOUR EMOTIONS.

YOU ARE THE
GATEKEEPER OF
YOUR WORLD. YOU
CHOOSE WHAT AND
WHO YOU LET INTO
YOUR LIFE.

DRAW THE UNEXPECTED

FINISH EACH OF THE ILLUSTRATIONS BELOW, BUT NONE OF THEM CAN BE WHAT THEY ARE "SUPPOSED" TO BE. NO UMBRELLAS, CLOUDS, OR ICE CREAM CONES ALLOWED HERE!

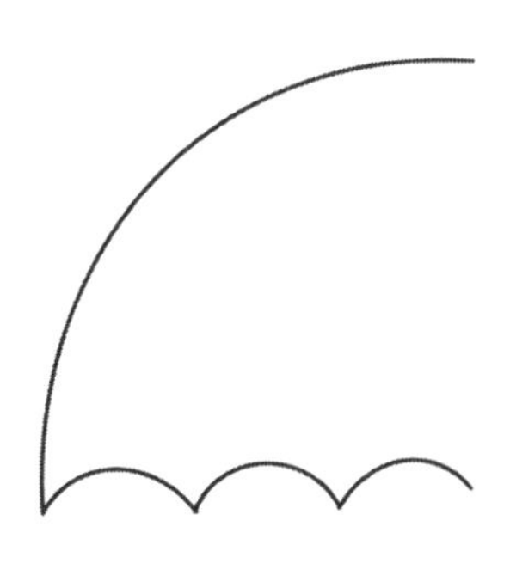

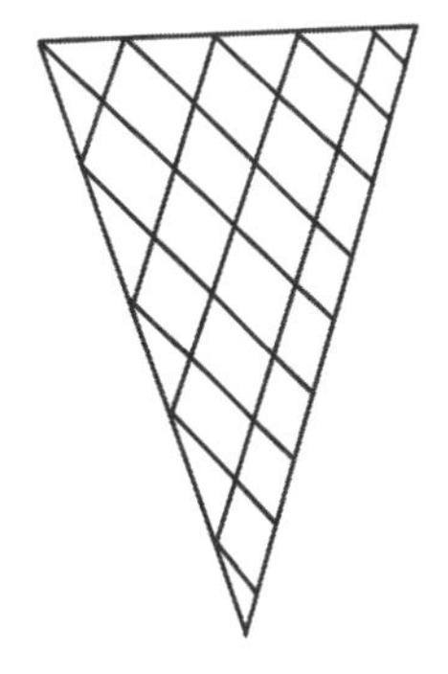

THERE IS NOTHING
YOU ARE REQUIRED
TO DO OR BE. JUST
EXISTING AS YOU
ARE IS ENOUGH.
ALWAYS.

BUILD A BUCKET LIST

FILL OUT THE BOXES BELOW WITH THINGS YOU'D LIKE TO DO IN THE FUTURE. MAKE A NOTE TO COME BACK TO THIS IN FIVE TO TEN YEARS TO SEE WHAT YOU'VE CHECKED OFF YOUR LIST.

I WANT TO LEARN ABOUT...

I WANT TO VISIT...

I WANT TO LIVE IN (PLACE / STYLE OF HOME / ETC.)...

I WANT TO BE THE KIND OF PERSON WHO...

I WANT TO TRY...

I WANT TO CREATE...

I WANT TO FEEL...

TODAY'S DATE: ________________ I WILL COME BACK ON: ________________

ACKNOWLEDGMENTS

A HUGE "THANK YOU!" GOES OUT TO EVERYONE WHO PLAYED A ROLE IN BRINGING INTO THE MOMENT TO LIFE.

TO MY AMAZING FAMILY – YOUR UNWAVERING SUPPORT FOR MY IDEAS AND YOUR EFFORTS TO HELP ME STAY IN THE MOMENT MEAN THE WORLD TO ME. THANK YOU FOR EVERYTHING.

TO MY INCREDIBLE AGENT, MONIKA VERMA, AND MY AWESOME EDITOR, LAUREN APPLETON – THANK YOU FOR GUIDING MY IDEAS AND PROVIDING ENCOURAGEMENT. AND AN EXTRA THANKS FOR THE MONTHS AND MONTHS SPENT WORKING WITH ME ON THE TITLE! WE DID IT!

TO MY FRIENDS – YOUR KINDNESS AND COMPASSION DURING THE CREATION OF THIS BOOK HAVE MEANT SO MUCH TO ME, AND I'M FOREVER THANKFUL FOR THE WAYS YOU HELP BRING ME BACK TO THE MOMENT.

ABOUT THE AUTHOR

DANI DIPIRRO IS AN AUTHOR AND ARTIST RESIDING IN THE WASHINGTON, DC, SUBURBS. IN 2009, SHE CREATED THE WEBSITE POSITIVELYPRESENT.COM AS A PLATFORM TO SHARE HER INSIGHTS ON LIVING A MORE POSITIVE AND PRESENT LIFE.

DANI IS THE AUTHOR OF MANY BOOKS, INCLUDING OUT OF YOUR MIND: A JOURNAL AND COLORING BOOK TO DISTRACT YOUR ANXIOUS MIND AND GROW THROUGH IT: INSPIRATION FOR WEATHERING LIFE'S SEASONS, AMONG OTHERS.

FOR A DAILY DOSE OF DANI'S WORK, YOU CAN FIND HER ON INSTAGRAM @POSITIVELYPRESENT. TO LEARN MORE ABOUT DANI, VISIT POSITIVELYPRESENT.COM.